M000188659

PRACTICAL ATLANTEAN MAGIC

By the same author:
ATLANTIS: MYTH OR REALITY
ANCIENT EGYPT: THE SIRIUS CONNECTION
THE BOOK OF TALIMANTRAS
ELEMENTS OF THE GREEK TRADITION
ESSENTIAL WOMAN
THE LION PEOPLE
THE NINE LIVES OF TYO
OLYMPUS: AN EXPERIENCE IN SELF-DISCOVERY?
PRACTICAL CELTIC MAGIC
PRACTICAL EGYPTIAN MAGIC
PRACTICAL GREEK MAGIC
PRACTICAL TECHNIQUES OF PSYCHIC SELF-DEFENCE
THE PSYCHOLOGY OF HEALING
THE PSYCHOLOGY OF RITUAL
TIME: THE ULTIMATE ENERGY
THE WAY OF CARTOUCHE

PRACTICAL ATLANTEAN MAGIC

A Study of the Science, Mysticism and Theurgy of Ancient Atlantis

Murry Hope

The Aquarian Press

An Imprint of HarperCollins*Publishers*

The Aquarian Press
An Imprint of HarperCollins*Publishers*
77–85 Fulham Palace Road,
Hammersmith, London W6 8JB

Published by The Aquarian Press 1991
1 3 5 7 9 10 8 6 4 2

© Murry Hope 1991

Murry Hope asserts the moral right to
be identified as the author of this work

A CIP catalogue record for this book
is available from the British Library

ISBN 1 85538 0692

Typeset by Harper Phototypesetters Limited,
Northampton, England
Printed in Great Britain by
Billing & Sons Limited, Worcester

All rights reserved. No part of this publication may be
reproduced, stored in a retrieval system, or transmitted,
in any form or by any means, electronic, mechanical,
photocopying, recording or otherwise, without the prior
permission of the publishers.

CONTENTS

Introduction   9

1. The Evolution of Atlantis   11
2. The Birth of a Nation   27
3. Plato's Atlanteans   44
4. Atlantis – Where and When?   55
5. Atlantis – The Island Continent   72
6. The Peoples of Atlantis   85
7. Science in Atlantis   98
8. The Atlantean Religion   113
9. Magic/Occultism in Atlantis   131
10. The Priests of Atlantis   152
11. Atlantis – Its Ultimate Fate   162
12. Will Atlantis Rise Again?   176

Bibliography   187
Index   190

DEDICATION

For Cynthia, who has been a loyal friend for so many years.

ACKNOWLEDGEMENTS

Acknowledgements and thanks are due to the following publishers and authors who have kindly granted me permission to use illustrations and quote from their books:

Dr An Pang Tsai of the Institute for Materials Research, Tohoku University, Japan, for permission to reproduce his excellent photograph of a quasi-crystal (originally reproduced in *Scientific American,* April 1991).

Penguin Books Ltd: *Archaic Egypt* by Prof W.B. Emery.

Inner Traditions International Ltd., Rochester, Vermont, USA: *Sacred Science* by R.A. Schwaller de Lubicz.

Readers Digest Association Ltd: *Great Illustrated Dictionary.*

The Pegasus Foundation: *Atlantis: Past and to Come* (Ed. S. Taylor).

Turnstone Books Ltd: *Maps of the Ancient Sea Kings* by Charles Hapgood and *Colony Earth* by Richard Mooney.

Bristol Classical Press: *Plato: The Atlantis Story* by Christopher Gill.

Aquarian Press Ltd: *The Occult Sciences in Atlantis* by Lewis Spence.

C.W. Daniel Co: *The Other Atlantis and Secrets of Lost Atland* by Robert Scrutton.

Warner Books, New York *Edgar Cayce on Atlantis* by Edgar Cayce.

Souvenir Press Ltd: *Colony Earth* by Richard Mooney.

Artwork by Martin Jones.

INTRODUCTION

ATLANTIS! A word that is evocative of a period long, long ago in the history of our planet, when a great civilization rose to a peak of achievement, only to meet its end in a watery grave. The preceding ages, and the factors that contributed to both its rise and its fall are, however, so deeply etched on the collective unconscious of *Homo sapiens*, that the very name is calculated to induce strong emotional responses ranging from warm and fond memories to outright fear.

Over the ages, and particularly in recent times, there have been those who have chosen to disregard the Atlantis story on supposed 'rational' grounds, relegating it to the realms of pure myth and superstition and going to absurd lengths to disprove it and discredit the accounts of such great philosophers as Plato, and the evidence offered by other scholars of erudition and distinction. But as any psychologist knows, fanatical disbelief is as much an indication of unbalanced thinking as excessive gullibility, true science demanding a fair assessment of the empirical evidence plus an open mind regarding logical theories and future discoveries. After all, it was not so long ago that Troy, like Atlantis, was seen only in the mythical context, and there are many other instances of similar finds that will be highlighted in the ensuing chapters.

The pragmatic pros and cons of the Atlantean saga have been well and truly dealt with in earlier works. My own book, *Atlantis: Myth or Reality?*, for example, examines the evidence available from all sources, including satellite photographic material, new geological information on former axis tilts, oceanographic charts of possible sites, and recent underwater discoveries. A fully comprehensive index of applicable material is also supplied, and appropriate historical references catalogued. However, my aim in this book is to approach the subject from a predominantly metaphysical angle, so although I will be including a certain amount of historical, geological and geographical data, the emphasis will be more on the mystical, psychological and psi aspects of the Atlantean phenomenon.

When dealing with a subject of this nature it should be always borne in mind that the dividing line between reality and fantasy is an extremely fine one, and to steer a steady course between the absurd and the prejudiced is no easy task. It inevitably falls to the metaphysician to walk the tightrope between reason and intuition, and a careful balance between right and left brain hemisphere input must therefore be aimed for at all times. As someone who was born with what are generally referred to as 'psychic' gifts, but who also has strong leanings towards science and psychology, I shall do my best to present a picture of Atlantis – its history, and the relevance of its message to today's world – from information gleaned via the sensitivity of many of those intuitively gifted mystics, seers and channellers with whom I have been privileged to work and study over the past forty years, and from my own occasional glimpses into the long, dead past. Some of my readers may see fit to disagree with these findings but others will, I know, *remember* as I and my associates have done, and with us shed tears of joy for what once was, and of sorrow at its tragic loss. And may the Old Ones guide my footsteps safely along this beautiful, inspiring, but chaotically seductive path.

1. THE EVOLUTION OF ATLANTIS

Atlantology, the name given in recent years to the specific study of the lost continent, enjoyed a popularity boost when Ignatius Donnelly's book *Atlantis – The Antediluvian World* was published in the last century. This work proved so popular that a poll taken by the British press at the time accorded the news value of Atlantis as second only to the Second Coming of Christ! So what is it about the legend of Atlantis that has so captured public imagination over the centuries? Since many believers in the Atlantis story have tended to rely upon their own intuition and far memory rather than empirical proof, the indication is surely that some catastrophic event of global proportions occurred at a point in the archaic past, the trauma of which has become deeply etched in the collective unconscious of mankind. What that event was and who and what were the people it most affected, constitutes the subject matter of the ensuing chapters. Intuition and psi accepted, however, it is sometimes a wise policy to play devil's advocate in these matters for, as we shall subsequently see, the name Atlantis is often erroneously bestowed on any memory of a magical past that carries Edenic or Utopian connotations, by people who are unfamiliar with the concept of parallel universes and similar phenomena.

Assuming that such a place as Atlantis did once exist, in what time context, as far as the known history of this planet is concerned, did this fabulous civilization rise to the unparalleled heights such eminent scholars as Plato would have us believe, and when did it take its final look at the benevolent sun that once blessed its fertile plains with two harvests a year? In order to obtain something even remotely near to the chronology concerned, we need to look firstly at the accepted history of the land masses of our planet, and secondly at the cosmic influences that prevailed during those early years in the history of *Homo sapiens*.

Early Land Masses
Geologists believe that prior to their separation some 200 million years ago all the continents of the world were grouped together in a single land mass, which is known as Pangaea (from the Greek meaning 'all earth'). At the end of the Palaeozoic era, Pangaea split into two sections, Gondwanaland, which is the name ascribed to the hypothetical southern portion, consisting of Africa, South America, India, Arabia, Australia, Madagascar, New Guinea, the Malay peninsular, Indonesia and Antarctica; and Lurasia, the northern portion, comprising North America, Greenland, Europe and Asia (excluding the Indian subcontinent). Lurasia itself split during the Mesozoic era, into North America and Eurasia. The German zoologist Ernst Haeckel saw Gondwanaland as being synonymous with the legendary continent of Mu or Lemuria, which we shall shortly be discussing, although it is more likely that Lemuria/Mu was much smaller, and probably lay in the region of, or near, the west coast of South America.

In 1912, Dr Alfred Wegener (1880–1930), a German geologist, first recognized the clues to be found in geological evidence to hand and put forward his theory of continental drift, which no one seemed to take very seriously at the time. Wegener postulated that during the Early Tertiary epoch (Tertiary – denoting, or formed in the first period of the Cenozoic era – see following graph) there was no wide expanse of water between the Old and New Worlds, but only a single, homogeneous continent, which later separated into the platforms now shown as the continents on modern maps. He also hypothesized that changes in the Earth's axial spin from time to time could bring about new directions of continental drift, and pointed to the westerly movements of the continents as evidence of this spin effect. In 1972, Dr Leon Knopoff and Dr A. Leed, of the University of California at Los Angeles, reported in *Science* the motion of the Earth's ten major crustal plates and confirmed the present tendency towards a westerly drift. Apparently, in the past the movements of the continents were northerly or southerly and unrelated to present spin.[1]

HOW LIFE HAS EVOLVED

The Earth's story, revealed by its rocks

The eras of the Earth have been well established by isotope dating in which the age of rocks is determined by the amount of radioactive-decay products they contain. Major divisions reflect changes in the positions of continents and the emergence of new forms of life.

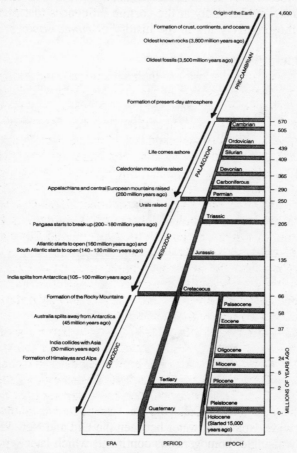

ERAS OF THE WORLD *Eras (and periods) are defined by life forms. Fossils in pre-Cambrian rocks are very rare. The Palaeozoic ("old life") saw the rise of invertebrates and amphibians. The Mesozoic ("middle life") was the age of reptiles. The Cenozoic ("recent life") is the age of mammals.*

Figure 1. The geological time scale of the earth's history according to *Reader's Digest Great Illustrated Dictionary*. Dates obtained by radiocarbon tests have, however, been questioned recently, when discrepancies were observed following comparisons made with dendrochronological (tree-ring) datings. It would appear that because the interplay of energies between the Earth and outer space have not remained constant, datings effected prior to 5300 BC should be considered as much earlier.

Nor are these authorities the only ones to have taken into account possible changes in the angles of the Earth's axial rotation. Jeffrey Goodman writes: 'One of the most important anomalies that pole shift can explain is the periodic reversal of the Earth's magnetic axis', and quotes Drs Allan Cox, Brent Dalrymple and Richard Doell, three of the United States Geographical Society's top scientists, as stating: 'After centuries of research the earth's magnetic field remains one of the best described and least understood of all planetary phenomena.'[3]

The above references to northerly or southerly continental drifts emphasize something I have always known instinctively, or 'remembered' as the case may be, that during the Atlantean epoch the Earth lay at a different angle in relation to the Sun, the poles and equator, and therefore the northern and southern hemispheres

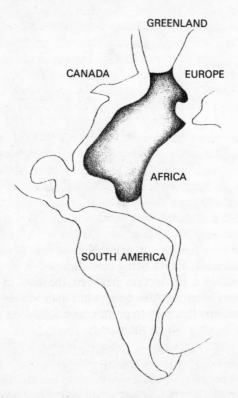

Figure 2. From the above it may be observed that the shelves do not match in the North Atlantic, although they accord with Wegener's theory further south.

were nowhere near their present position. This means that many of the lands that are now warm were then cool or cold, while parts that now enjoy temperate or even subtropical climates were under ice. There was, therefore, no world Ice Age as such, simply a shifting of the weather patterns according to the angle of the Earth's axis at any given time. But more of that later.

Wegener's theory has often been used as evidence against the existence of Atlantis in the Atlantic Ocean, but a closer look at how the western and eastern continents fit together serves to highlight a large portion of missing land. [4]

Mu/Lemuria

During a visit to India in 1868, Colonel James Churchward was allowed access to certain ancient religious documents that told of a vast continent called Mu, that once existed in the Pacific. This ancient land had apparently housed an advanced race which eventually colonized most of Asia, South America, Southern Europe, Asia Minor and North Africa. The name Mu, he tells us, means 'The Motherland', Lemuria being an identity later accorded to this hypothetical island continent by the British scientist P. Sclater, who believed that the lemur species originally evolved there.

Churchward insists that the Atlantean influence was quite distinct from the Mu-an, and gives several clues as to how the two can be distinguished. Since both cultures must, at some time in the remote past, have originated in either Gondwanaland or Lurasia, certain common cultural and magical links must have existed. I am inclined to associate Atlantis more with Lurasia, and Mu with Gondwanaland as Haeckel suggested, although there obviously must have been places and points in time at which both cultures intermingled; Egypt being one example. It is, therefore, necessary to effect a distinction between the two in order to pinpoint the areas of strong Atlantean rather than Mu-an influence in those civilizations that rose to prominence following the major upheavals that brought about their ends.

Since an archaic common source for both cultures is indicated, there are obviously many shared symbols and magical beliefs, although just how much influence this Pacific civilization had upon its Atlantic successor will constitute part of our enquiry. One of the main Mu-an symbols to be incorporated into Atlantiana was undoubtedly the equidistant cross, used to depict the Primary Four. According to Churchward's information, the Mu-ans were monotheistic, since they conceived of a single Creator who gave Seven Great Commands which were carried out by the Sacred Four, whom I would see in terms of the four basic elemental principles, represented in magic/metaphysics by Fire, Air, Water and Earth, and in science by the four combined energies that some scientists opine will constitute the basis of a Grand Unified Theory – the electromagnetic force, strong and weak nuclear forces, and gravity.

Sun worship obviously featured prominently in Mu-an religion, although it has been suggested that the Sun was seen purely as a physical manifestation of a single, multifaceted divinity. The second most prominent symbol to find its way, via Mu, into Atlantean mysticism was undoubtedly the winged disk, which was later to become one of the major insignia of the Atlantean High Priests. When examining Mu-an symbology, I was particularly struck by the absence of lunar references, the emphasis being essentially solar, the reason for which will shortly be seen.

So, assuming that Mu enjoyed a pre-Atlantean existence, what was the nature of its culture; what caused its destruction; and when

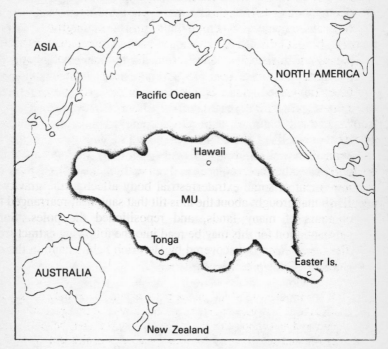

Figure 3. The geological position of Mu according to Churchward.

Figure 4. Cited by Churchward as one of the earliest solar symbols, which his researches indicated to be of Mu-an origin, and therefore probably dating back to 35000 BC or earlier.

Figure 5. **Above right**. According to Churchward, this was the Royal Escutcheon of Mu.

did all this take place? According to Churchward's researches, the ancient Mu-ans were a highly advanced people who latterly interbred with the primitive races they colonized. Their continent covered nearly half of the Pacific Ocean, and its eventual demise was caused by the escape of gases from vast underground caverns deep beneath the sea which had, until then, maintained sufficient pressure to hold the land in position. Upon their eventual collapse the land they had been supporting went down with them. Churchward substantiates his theories with various premises, some of which are scientifically viable and others not. But what we do know is that when Mu sank, an immense northern area was also submerged, plus smaller areas to the west. My own contention is that events of this nature do not normally occur without some external cosmic intervention, and that it was the movement of some extraterrestrial body affecting the gravity of Earth that brought about the axis tilt that sank Mu, rearranged the contours of many lands, and repositioned the poles. Some substantiation for this may be read into the following extract from *The Lhasa Record* discovered by Heinrich Schliemann in the old Buddhist Temple of Lhasa, Tibet:

When the star of Bal fell on the place where now is only the sky and sea, the seven cities with their golden gates and transparent temples, quivered and shook like the leaves in a storm; and, behold, a flood of fire and smoke arose from the palaces. Agonies and cries of the multitude filled the air. They sought refuge in their temples and citadels, and the wise Mu – the *Hieratic Ra Mu* – arose and said to them: did I not predict all this? And the women and men in their precious stones and shining garments lamented 'Mu, save us!' And Mu replied 'You shall all die together with your servants and your riches, and from your ashes new nations shall arise. If they forget they are superior not because of what they put on but what they put out the same will befall them.' Flames and smoke choked the words of Mu: the land and its inhabitants were torn to pieces and swallowed up by the depths. [5]

And when did all this take place? One valuable document that we have inherited from the Mayans may provide a clue. This is the *Codex Troanus*, which is preserved in the British Museum and estimated from the form of writing to be between 1,500 and 5,000 years old. The lands referred to are Mu and Moud, while the date given for the occurrence is 8,060 years before the Codex was compiled. The text runs thus:

> On the sixth day of Can, in the eleventh Muluc in the month of Zac, occurred dreadful earthquakes and continued until the thirteenth Chuen. The land of Clay Hills Mu and the land Moud were the victims. They were shaken twice and in the night suddenly disappeared. The earth crust was continually raised and lowered in many places by the subterranean forces until it could not resist such stresses, and many countries became separated one from another by deep crevices. Finally both provinces could not resist such tremendous stresses and sank in the ocean together with 64,000,000 inhabitants. It occurred 8,060 years ago. [6]

This Codex also refers to Mu as the birthplace of the sacred mysteries, *The Land of Kui, the motherland of the gods*, which was confirmed by the renowned Egyptologist Sir Gardner Wilkinson, who wrote: 'Kui-land, or the land of Kui, according to the Mayan language, was the birthplace of the goddess Maya, the mother of the gods – and of man.' [7] Another authenticated document which confirms the Mu tale is the *Codex Cortesianus*, now in the National Museum of Madrid, which would appear to be roughly the same age as the *Troanus*, although the language employed is more mystical and contains a degree of obscure symbology. A portion of the text runs:

> By his strong arm Homen caused the earth to tremble after sunset and during the night *Mu, the country of the hills of earth, was submerged.*

Mu, the life of the basin (seas), was submerged by Homen during the night.

The place of the dead *rulers* is now lifeless, it moves no more, after having *twice* jumped from its foundations: the king of the deep, while forcing his way out, has shaken it up and down, has killed it, has submerged it.

Twice Mu jumped from her foundations; it was then *sacrificed* by *fire*. It *burst* while being shaken up and down violently by earthquakes. By kicking it, the wizard that makes all things move like a mass of worms, *sacrificed* it that very night.[8] (my italics)

The idea of a continent sinking overnight has strained the credulity of many a scientist whose particular discipline has insisted in the 'steady state' concept of world evolution. However, the advent of chaos science has brought about radical changes in scientific thinking regarding those cataclysmic premises that were previously seen purely in the mythological or science-fiction context. Or, as one scientist puts it, 'WHERE CHAOS BEGINS, classical science stops.'[9]

Possible Datings for the Mu-an Catastrophe

Churchward's case for the existence of Mu was built entirely around two sets of ancient tablets: the Naacal tablets, which he discovered in India, and a large collection of stone tablets discovered by William Niven in Mexico. Although his researches are mainly concerned with the sunken Pacific continent, Churchward does make the occasional reference to the records of ancient Western cultures and fully acknowledges the existence of Atlantis as a separate and distinct continent with a vastly different influence from that of Mu. His dates for the Mu-an catastrophe are based on findings in the mausoleum of Cay, high priest and eldest son of King Can, at Chichen Itza, Yucatan. These include a carving of a serpent with twelve heads, which carried an inscription to the effect that the serpent symbolized the twelve Mayax dynasties that had reigned prior to the Can, their combined reigns covering a period of 18,000 years. According to the *Codex Troanus*, the last Can king lived some 16,000 years ago, and this figure, added to 18,000 gives us the figure of 34,000, or approximately 32000 BC. Since the length of the Can dynasty is not clearly defined there could well have been monarchs reigning previously to this, so Churchward estimates an approximate time of 33000 BC for the reign of the first Mayax king. Mayax, he tells us, was one of Mu's major colonies, having advanced to colonial status from a mere settlement, so overall Mu could be seen to date back to between 45000 and 50000 BC. Some of these figures, notably the 18,000 year reign of the dynasties of kings, also receive confirmation in the Chinese book *Tchi*, while Japanese, Hindu and Egyptian records also serve to verify the antiquity of this pre-Atlantean culture.

In more recent times, the British scientist, Blandford, expressed the opinion that both physical geography and paleontology unanimously confirmed the existence of Lemuria from the so-called 'Permian' epoch until the end of the Miocene Period. This seems a little early to me since, according to geological and anthropological sources, the development and increase of mammals did not take place until the Cenozoic Period. Other scientists, however, have dated the Lemurian catastrophe nearer 15000 BC, which coincides with Hapgood's assessment of the beginning of a sizeable shift in the Earth's crust. This would have given the Atlanteans some 6,000 or 7,000 years in which to build up their civilization to the status it achieved prior to its disappearance. Lemuria has also been seen as synonymous with Gondwanaland, which has served to perplex Braghine and other Atlantologists, as the early legends state that the population of Gondwanaland did not know the Moon! The Mu-an and Atlantean cataclysms, however, occurred at vastly different periods in pre-history as later chapters will show, and although their causes are still debatable, ancient records, aided by modern technology, are helping researchers to 'sort the wheat from the chaff'. According to an article in the *National Geographic* entitled 'The Search for Modern Humans', a carved body of a man – the world's earliest known anthropomorphic figure, which pushes back in time evidence of human ability to create symbols – has been excavated at the 32,000-year level in a cave in Hohlenstein, West Germany. Years later, museum officials were presented with a beautifully carved ivory lion muzzle that had been found in the same cave: it fitted the statuette perfectly.[10] This could possibly be seen as an indication of the Mu-an influence in Europe, although there might well be some other explanation that will unfold with time.

Stellar Influences
Astrological Ages are believed to exert a strong influence on events that take place during their periods of ascendancy. Tracing these back to the times of Mu and Atlantis may therefore serve to throw

some light on the cosmic transformative energies at work on Gaia during the periods in question. For those unfamiliar with Professor James Lovelock's Gaia Hypothesis, it conceives of the planet Earth as a living, highly intelligent, self-regulating entity in its own right, which Lovelock has chosen to refer to by the old Greek mythological name of Gaia (see *Gaia – A New Look at Life on Earth* and *The Ages of Gaia*, Oxford University Press, 1982). Not all ancient peoples referred to Earth in the feminine context, however; the Egyptians, for example, saw our planet as the male Geb, husband of Nut, the Sky.

Just as we, as individuals, are influenced by the movements of the planets and other heavenly bodies in our own solar system, so too is our Earth, be she Gaia, Geb, or whomever. So, in order to see where Mu and Atlantis fit into the astrological scheme of things, a cursory glance at the dates concerned will undoubtedly prove helpful.

The 'Great Year' is the name given to the period of time (roughly 25,826 years) taken by the pole of the Earth's axis to complete an entire cycle around the ecliptic, the sun's apparent path among the stars when viewed against the background of the constellations. The gradual changing of direction of the Earth's axis is known as the Precession of the Equinoxes. Each year the point in space where the sun crosses the celestial equator (referred to by astronomers as the vernal equinox and by astrologers as Aries), when viewed against the background of the constellations, is seen from the Earth as slightly behind the position it occupied the previous year. Consequently, the nearest star to which the axis points, known as the Pole Star, changes through the ages. Confusion arises from the fact that the constellations have the same names as the signs of the zodiac. Astronomers, therefore, tend to look askance when those interested but untutored in the subtleties of astrology speak of being 'born under the star sign of Leo', for example. The signs of the zodiac (the word zodiac comes from the Greek, and means 'circle of animals') are not synonymous with the constellations with whom they share a name, a fact that should be borne in mind when one is thinking of astrological ages. The constellations that are marked on stellar charts as groups of stars are purely points of reference, since the light from these bodies may have taken hundreds of light years to reach us, during which they may well have long since moved to different locations.

The Great Year

Just as our year is divided into twelve months, the Great Year is similarly divided into twelve ages. These are the periods of time when the equinox is judged to have been against the background of each of the twelve constellations that appear to lie roughly around the ecliptic. We are told that these periods cannot be reckoned with any real degree of accuracy, but are roughly 2,000 or so years each. Nor can the commencement of each period be fixed, because the boundaries of the constellations are not clearly defined. As the movement is backwards from the end of the constellation to its beginning, the periods of time are in backward order through the signs. The last 2,000 years are seen by astrologers to have exhibited characteristics that are decidedly Piscean, while the age into which we are just entering is that of Aquarius. Each Age is seen as exerting certain psychological influences that manifest strongly in those civilizations that flourish under its ethos, and some signs, it would seem, are more prone to becoming the tools of evolutionary quantum leaps than others, as we shall shortly see. It is during these chaotic manifestations of cosmic influences that major catastrophes of the kind that sent Mu and Atlantis to their watery resting places would appear to take place. Working backwards, the picture therefore appears thus:

The Piscean Age: (c.60 BC–AD 1995). Among other factors, the deeply responsive and secretive sign of Pisces is associated with the kind of religious collectives that are motivated by emotional appeal. The glyph of the Fishes pulling against each other directs the mind to consider the psychological and spiritual conflicts that might arise from the watery and fertile depths of the deep unconscious, that could be seen to have characterized the past 2,000 years.

The Arien Age: (c.2000 BC–60 BC). A period of exploration and conquest, when empires rose and fell, as might be expected, Mars being the ruler of Aries.

The Taurean Age: (c.4000 BC–2000 BC). This embraced the civilizations of Minoa and early Egypt. The bull figured prominently in the rites, religions and cultures of this era.

The Geminian Age: (c.6000 BC–4000 BC). This is frequently referred to by astrologers as relating to twin-god cults, but I am inclined to view it more as a period of confusion or choice, when humanity was poised between two factors. This could be translated as the matrist/patrist dilemma, the onset of the heroic cults or simply a period of movement, communication, and the development of new thinking processes.

The Cancerian Age: (*c.*8000 BC–6000 BC). This watery sign is ruled by the Moon. I see it as encompassing the Silver Age of Greek mythology, and having a definite bearing on the Flood, and the sinking of Atlantis, although I am at variance with those authorities who designate the Atlantean cataclysm as having taken place near the beginning of this sign.

The Leonine Age: (*c.*10000 BC–8000 BC). This was the last great age of Atlantis, the Golden Age of the Greeks, when Cronus (Time?) ruled and the continent prospered.

The Virgoan Age: (*c.*12000 BC–10000 BC). In my opinion, the best period in the whole of Atlantean history. It embraced a time when the arts and sciences – medicine, astronomy, sonics and physics in particular – flourished in the 'Old Country', (a term often used affectionately by confirmed believers). The feminine principle was fully acknowledged, and the accent was more on spiritual than material and corporeal pleasures.

The Libran Age: (*c.*14000 BC–12000 BC). This was the age of rebalancing that followed directly after the sinking of Mu and the drastic changes that occurred in the contours of the body of Gaia worldwide. It was during this Age that the Atlantean civilization was born, following the island continent's break from those mainlands to which it was originally attached. This gave the isolated pockets of culture a chance to develop their own distinctive evolutionary pattern, and accommodate the evolutionary quantum jump that was to affect the future physical and mental growth of *Homo sapiens* for centuries ahead.

The Scorpionic Age: (*c.*16000 BC–14000 BC). This was probably the age in which Mu or Lemuria met its catastrophic end. Scorpio is believed by astrologers to be ruled by the planet Pluto, whose chthonic influences are associated with the cycle of elimination and regeneration, or death and rebirth. Scorpio (and, therefore, Pluto) dominates the early to middle part of the month of November, and it is interesting to note that in Japan, Peru, Central America, India, the Pacific Islands, Australia, ancient Persia and parts of Egypt – all places believed to have been colonies of Mu – the beginning of November was held sacred to the 'ancient ancestors'. [11] A remnant of this belief has survived to this day in the various Pagan Festivals such as Halloween, the Celtic Samhain, and the Christian observance of All Souls Day. The Egyptian Set or Setekh, god of Chaos, was also associated with the sign of Scorpio, Set's encapsulation of the body of Osiris in the chest which was then cast into the sea (via the Nile?) having taken place on 'the 17th day of the month of Athyr when the Sun was in Scorpio in the 28th year of Osiris's reign'. Perhaps the legend is referring to an actual happening, when the ordered rule of the Osirian dynasty was toppled by certain seismic and allied occurrences (cataclysms) that ultimately destroyed his kingdom, leaving it in chaos? But then it must be remembered that we are dealing with two cataclysms or major axis tilts here, the earlier of which would appear to have Scorpionic associations while the latter connects with the Age of Cancer – *both water signs*.

Opinions differ as to whether major transformations of a cataclysmic nature occur at the onset or during the final days of an astrological Age. I am inclined to favour the latter although my choice is not based purely on intuition. A study of the data available on previous axis tilts, plus chronological records from legend and folklore worldwide tend to support this idea.

Churchward's researches into the beliefs and culture of the ancient Mu-ans show a marked inclination towards ancestor worship, remnants of which are still to be found in those areas that they originally colonized. The Polynesians, for example, place great significance on the power and importance of their ancestors, as do many Chinese to this day. I recall a particular instance when I was attending a major London psychic festival and was approached by a venerable Chinese gentleman who sought my advice on a private matter. He must have been satisfied with the little help I was able to give him as he thanked me and added: 'I know that you, too, have many problems to face in the future, but you are fortunate in that you have powerful ancestors, who will help you to overcome them.'

A recent study of quantum mechanics has opened my eyes to the scientific significance of this remark, and enabled me to understand how Truth is a constant factor that exists at many levels or frequencies; it is only in our interpretation of the details that confusion (Chaos) exerts its influence and our faiths fragment. A shattered hologram may shed many fragments, each of which is perceived by the beholder as unique, and interpreted according to his or her *own particular level of cosmic awareness* or, to use a more familiar term, *soul age*.

Churchward insists that the original Mu-ans were a highly evolved race with technological and artistic skills equal to anything we have today. The same has also been said of the Atlanteans, while similar views have been expressed by other writers and researchers when commenting on finds that indicate an evolutionary retrogression among the peoples of Earth resulting from some major catastrophe and accompanying climatic changes. The idea of highly advanced prehistoric races has spawned a host of premises concerning the possibility of genetic mutations effected from beings from other parts of the universe. Many well known writers have enjoyed a heyday in this field, and while the sci-fi angle should not be ignored, there is always the possibility that at least one theory could be correct. Robert K. G. Temple's book, *The Sirius Mystery*, ranks among the more logical of the books I have encountered on the subject, although he tends to limit his area of enquiry to certain epochs, when there would appear to be just as much evidence to support the arrival of extra terrestrials at much earlier periods in Gaia's youth.

One of the arguments often put forward by sceptics against the possibility of highly advanced races existing in prehistory is the archaeological, and other empirical evidence, of the primitive lifestyle of Stone Age man. The facetiousness of this argument lies in the fact that one can still find isolated tribes living under Stone Age conditions only a few hundred miles away from a highly modern metropolis. Churchward insists that any great nation that suddenly finds itself denied the facilities of civilization is likely to revert to degeneracy and savagery, and will soon assume the upper hand in situations where knowledge of the higher arts, sciences and humanities have slipped slowly into myth and legend. His words are confirmed by Plato in the ensuing chapter (see page 35).

Not all of the Mu-an influence was lost, however; and just as great nations have arisen from the colonies of earlier empires, so Mu seeded what was eventually to mutate into one of the strangest, and probably most fascinating legends of all times, that of the lost continent of Atlantis.

Endnotes
1. *Science*, 31 August 1973, No. 181, pp.803–9.
2. *Reader's Digest Great Illustrated Dictionary*, Vol. 1, p.700.
3. Goodman, J. *The Earthquake Generation*, p.166.
4. Hope, M. *Atlantis: Myth or Reality?* pp.73–5.
5. Churchward, J. *The Lost Continent of Mu*, p.80.
6. Braghine A. *The Shadow of Atlantis*, pp.30–31.
7. Wilkinson, G. *Manners and Customs*, Vol. III, p.70.
8. Op. cit. Churchward, pp.78–9.

9. Gleick, J. *Chaos: Making a New Science*, p.3.
10. John J. Putnam. 'The Search for Modern Humans', *National Geographic,* Vol. 174, no.4, October 1988, pp. 111–13.
11. Op. cit. Churchward, pp.310–11.

2. THE BIRTH OF A NATION

The Separation from Mu

The earth tremors and accompanying cosmological and seismic phenomena that sent Mu to the depths of the Pacific Ocean also caused mountain ranges to rise, elevating cities that were previously at sea level to the tops of newly formed high plateaux or mountains, thus isolating the inhabitants from the survivors in the lower regions. Evidence of this is to be found in South and Central America, and researchers are only just beginning to piece together a picture of the original races that built and inhabited these strange, hidden cities. This same cataclysm also fragmented many lands, altering established seaboards and creating islands where none had previously existed. There must have been a period in the archaic past when what was later to become the island continent of Atlantis was joined to both America and Europe. Geological and legendary evidence would seem to suggest that its first break was from the latter, in which case the Atlanteans of the Libran Age would probably have inherited more of the characteristics of the northern Mu-an colonies than of the original Motherland.

Churchward maintains that the first Mu-ans to colonize America were blond-whites, and that these fair people were driven from their land by another white race of 'more swarthy complexion – brunettes.'[1] Churchward tells us that these fair people 'sailed in their ships to a far off land in the direction of the rising sun – east -- and there settled in the northern part of Europe – Scandinavia of today.'[2] What is more likely is that these northern Mu-an colonizers pursued a path across land links that existed in those times, and it is logical to assume this tribe of ancient colonists to be the one that came to inhabit the lands that latterly broke away from the northern mainlands to become the island continent of Atlantis. When describing these Mu-an journeys, however, Churchward failed to take into account the fact that since the Earth's axis was at a different angle from what it is today, any ideas of north, south, east or west could not possibly apply. Ancient Egyptian records confirm that the sun has risen and set in several different locations, which have varied according to our planet's position in relation to the Sun, a fact that can be verified in the writings of Professor Charles Hapgood, in physicist Peter Warlow's book *The Reversing Earth*, science editor John Waite's *Pole Shift*, and from satellite pictures taken from outside our Earth.[3]

An Archaic Vestige?

A BBC television programme entitled *From the Heart of the World*, that was shown in early December 1990, featured the Kogi, an isolated tribe of Indians who occupy the higher slopes of a mountain in northern Columbia, the nearest town to which is Santa Mata. The Elders, or holy men and women, who are known as 'mamas', wished to give a message from the 'older brothers' (themselves) to the 'younger brothers' (the rest of the world), concerning the dangers of pursuing the present policy of the rape of Gaia (e.g. the destruction of the rain forest and the continual removal of minerals, gases, etc. from the Earth).

In spite of their apparently primitive lifestyle, these gentle people were the custodians of a profound and highly enlightened philosophy which conceived of the equality of all living things, to which respect should therefore be equally accorded. Film maker Alan Ereira was allowed to enter Kogi territory so that they could record their message for the rest of us to hear and, we hope, respond to. Otherwise, who knows what might befall us?

Ereira's camera team was permitted to photograph some of the strange ruins of a city, built by the Kogi's distant ancestors, which showed evidence of an advanced culture, the technology of which had obviously been long since lost and forgotten. All that remained was the ancient wisdom and the sparse threads of a philosophy that was still followed to the book, albeit without full understanding of what many of the original teachings and precepts were really all about. Following their gentle but firm admonition of the nefarious activities of modern society in its desecration of 'the mother' (Gaia), the Kogi returned once more to the higher regions of their sacred mountain, where they would immediately undertake a long rite to purify them of any negative energies that may have contaminated them spiritually (or physically, maybe?) during their brief visit to 'civilization'.

This programme provided the matter for subsequent discussion among both Greens and non-Greens, and as far as Mu and Atlantis are concerned, the question inevitably arose as to whether the profundity of the philosophy they had inherited from their forefathers was of Mu-an or Atlantean origin or, perhaps, a blending of both? Since the Atlanteans colonized those parts fairly extensively, the latter probably applies. While watching this programme, and observing the obvious sensitivity and sincerity of these simple people, both I and my colleagues could not help but think of how our own antecedents could be thus reduced should a similar fate strike us in this present day and age.

The Atlantean Breakaway

This is but one tiny, living example of a link with the archaic past. There may be others; genetic, perhaps? I think yes. But let us first take a trip back in time to the period directly following the sinking of Mu, when the Atlantean island continent found itself completely isolated from the mainlands to which it had once been attached. Now, views as to this attachment vary with different researchers. Lewis Spence conceived of Atlantis as originally being a much larger land mass than Plato described (see pages 36, 45-9, 72), which split into two sections, the second of which he named Antillia (see Figure 6). Spence's placing of Antillia closer to the American coastline also makes sense, as we shall see. Regarding timing he tells us:

> . . . that these two island continents and the connecting chain of islands persisted until late Pleistocene times, at which epoch (about 25,000 years ago, or the beginning of the post-glacial epoch) Atlantis seems to have experienced further disintegration. Final disaster appears to have overtaken Atlantis about 10000 BC. Antillia, on the other hand, seems to have survived until a much more recent period and still persists fragmentally in the Antillean Group or West India islands.)[4]

I am not in agreement with Spence on this issue, however. I tend to see Plato's Atlantis as the later survivor, and the Antillian fragment relating to an earlier cataclysm that left a series of islands stretching into the Atlantic between the American coastline and the Atlantean mainland. American Indian and South and Central American legends would appear to support this theory. It should also be borne in mind that Atlantis, like Greenland, Scandinavia and parts of North America were all originally attached to the old Lurasian land mass and, taking into account the different positions of poles and equator, we could be dealing with a picture that varies considerably from that which we now see on our world maps.

Assuming the Mu/Lemuria catastrophe to have occurred in the latter part of the Age of Scorpio, which, for arguments sake we could assess to be somewhere around 14000 BC, the period immediately following this must obviously have been one of chaos and confusion. During this time, those survivors who found themselves domiciled on the newly formed continent endeavoured to pick up the pieces and reform themselves into what was

Figure 6. Lewis Spence's placing of the two islands.

Figure 7. Chaos/Order sequence.

eventually to become a highly civilized society. As chaos science affirms, Chaos in any of its many manifestations is eventually self-organizing, and the sine-waves of evolution would appear to follow this universal pattern with a deal of precision. During my early days as a music student my teacher was careful to point out, in explaining to me the mechanics of the human voice, how the Chaos-Order sequence manifested in the evolution of singing. This she defined in terms of a wave process of progression and retrogression, the latter, however, never quite reaching the original point. Taken as an overall picture occupying a period of time the progress is, of course, quite obvious, although if only one of these waves is visible at a time the retrogressive aspects could be read as disaster areas.

And so it is with the evolution of a planet. At the nadir of a retrogressive stage an evolutionary quantum jump usually occurs, which acts as a spur for the next forward impulse. This would appear to be what took place following the sinking of Mu, and Gaia's subsequent rearrangement of her body. However, according to arcane tradition no catastrophe ever occurs without all living creatures being forewarned in some way of its impending approach. And so it was prior to the sinking of Mu. Here is a short extract from a wisdom teaching on Atlantis channelled through Tony Neate back in the 1950s and given to a group called *The Atlanteans*, of which I was privileged to be a founder member along with Tony:

> Shortly before the continent of Mu was due to be affected by cataclysms, certain highly evolved spirits incarnated into Mu-an bodies. As these bodies grew to adulthood the wisdom of their spirits commenced to manifest and they found they were considerably more advanced in understanding than those around them. The submerged continent we call Atlantis was also part of the Mu-an empire at the time, and it was to this section of land that the aforementioned people made their way. As they advanced in life they recognized each other and banded together. They saw that things were not as they should

be so they decided to set up a community of their own in a part of the land that was uninhabited. Of course those parts of any land that are rich and healthy are not usually left untenanted, even by man as he was in those days, and the piece of land, or peninsular, upon which the early Atlanteans settled was damp, cold and unfriendly . . .

It was shortly after the early Atlanteans had settled upon this rather inhospitable piece of land and were trying bravely to make the best of a bad job that a giant catastrophe occurred, causing the face of the Earth to change yet again. The magnetic balance between the planets in the solar system was disturbed. The results were terrifying: a whole portion of a continent sank beneath what you now know as the Pacific ocean, the remaining land masses were split into smaller continents and the portion of land that the new Atlanteans had settled upon broke away from the main land mass. Due to the new position of planet Earth in relation to the Sun, climatic conditions throughout the world were changed: these first Atlanteans found they had acquired a bright, sunny land in exchange for the damp, marshy one, although, of course, the three zones of Atlantis differed according to their position in relation to what was then the Equator. [5]

Those that had been forewarned were, therefore, forearmed with the knowledge necessary for their survival, with which they had probably been programmed prior to entering incarnation. The question that is bound to arise from this is, who were these 'evolved spirits' and from which neck of the cosmic woods did they hail? Occultists and mystics have been ruminating on this one for centuries, and all sorts of suggestions have been put forward. Information that has come down to us from ancient Egyptian records in particular suggests the binary star Sirius as the most likely candidate although, no doubt, those incarnate among us who feel stronger affinities with, say, Orion, Aldebaran or Auriga might think differently. My own belief, which I share with Schwaller de Lubicz, Robert K. G. Temple and several other scholars and researchers is that our solar system was seeded from Sirius, and that this binary star has played a major role in the history of our own world from the time of its commencement. Although I am given to understand that there was another stellar race involved in the Mu-an epoch, Atlantis, like ancient Egypt, carried strong Siriun energies that latecomers to its shores found difficult, if not impossible, to handle. This will be covered in more detail in later chapters.

And so the Age of Scorpio gave way to the rebalancing energies of Libra, and the Atlantean survivors commenced the task of building a civilization, the likes of which has never been equalled to this day. At this point it is essential to bear in mind that the Age of Libra occupied some 2,000 years or more; so did the Age of Virgo and likewise the Ages of Leo and Cancer. This adds up to 8,000 years, or between 6,000 and 8,000 years if one agrees with Plato's dating of 9,000 or thereabouts for the final sinking of Atlantis. Plato's Atlantis would appear to relate very much to the Age of Leo, the latter part, maybe, since, in spite of the excellence of which he speaks, there were obvious signs of degeneracy. The Bull cults, for example, possibly were acquired from the Minoan-influenced mainlands rather than the opposite as some scholars have suggested. What I do wish to emphasize at this point is that a period as long as 6,000 years or more (assuming a year in those days to have been of similar duration to the 365 days we observe today) must obviously have evidenced many changes in its cultural, political and religious structure. So, comparing Plato's latter-day Atlantis with the conditions existing, say, 5,000 years earlier, would be comparable to making a comparison between modern-day Egypt and the Egypt of 3000 BC. So what *did* Plato have to say about the Atlantis that met its watery end in Neptune's green caverns? This seems an appropriate place to accord the great philosopher his first hearing.

The *Critias* and *Timaeus*

It has mainly been due to Plato that the Atlantis legend has been kept alive over the centuries, the two works in which it features, the *Critias* and the *Timaeus*, providing a fertile ground for polemic among classical scholars and laypersons alike. It is possible that one of the main problems as far as the historical accuracy of these accounts is concerned can be blamed on Plato, or his informants, as his texts show a degree of confusion concerning a war that supposedly took place between the ancient Athenians and a marauding sea-people to whom Plato refers as Atlanteans. However, these sea-people are believed by some authorities to have been ancient Frisians, whose lands in the North Sea are now estimated to have sunk around 5000 BC, and whose ancient records we will be considering later in this chapter. For those interested in the finer details, the subject matter receives a scholarly analysis in Professor Christopher Gill's *Plato: The Atlantis Story* (see Bibliography). Since the *Critias* and *Timaeus* are lengthy works, I shall commit what is often viewed in critique as the heinous crime of selecting only those passages appropriate to my particular approach to the subject, referring the more dedicated student (with a knowledge of Greek) to the aforementioned worthy Professor, and the less erudite to my own book *Atlantis: Myth or Reality*, which contains a fuller version of Plato's original text. As might be expected there are several translations available, and the one I have chosen is from Ignatius Donnelly's book *Atlantis: The Antediluvian World* which, while it might not be the most up to date, is sufficiently close to the Greek original to merit inclusion in any book dealing exclusively with the Atlantis material.

The introductory text commences as follows:

Critias: Then listen, Socrates, to a strange tale, which is, however, certainly true, as Solon, who was the wisest of the seven sages, declared. He was a relative and great friend of my great-grandfather, Dropidas, as he himself says in several of his poems, and Dropidas told Critias, my grandfather, who remembered, and told us . . .

I will tell an old-world story which I heard from an aged man; for Critias was, as he said, at that time nearly ninety years of age, and I was about ten years of age . . .

At the head of the Egyptian Delta, where the river Nile divides, there is a certain district which is called the district of Sais, and it is the city from which Amasis the king was sprung. And the citizens have a deity who is their foundress: she is called in the Egyptian tongue Neith, which is asserted by them to be the same which the Hellenes call Athene. Now the citizens of this city are great lovers of the Athenians, and say that they are in some way related to them. Thither came Solon, who was received by them with great honour; and he asked the priests, who were most skillful in such matters, about antiquity, and made the discovery that neither he nor any Hellene knew anything worth mentioning about the times of old. On one occasion, when he was drawing them on to speak of antiquity, he began to tell about the most ancient things in our part of the world – about Phoroneus, who is called 'the first'; and about Niobe; and, after the Deluge, to tell of the lives of Ducalion and Pyrrha, and he traced the genealogy of their descendants, and attempted to reckon how many years old were the events of which he was speaking, and to give the dates. Thereupon, one of the priests, who was of very great age, said: 'O Solon, Solon, you Hellenes are but children, and there is never an old man who is an Hellene.' Solon, hearing this, said: 'What do you mean?' 'I mean to say,' he replied, 'that in mind you are all young; there is no old opinion handed down among you by ancient tradition, nor any science which is hoary with age. And I will tell you the reason of this: there have been, and there will be again, many destructions of mankind arising out of many causes. There is

a story which even you have preserved, that once upon a time
Phaeton, the son of Helios, having yoked his steeds to his father's
chariot, because he was not able to drive them in the path of his father,
burnt up all that was upon the earth, and was himself destroyed by
a thunderbolt. Now, this has the form of a myth, but really signified
a declination of the bodies moving around the earth and in the
heavens, and a great conflagration of things upon the earth occurring
at long intervals of time: when this happens those who live upon the
mountains and in dry and lofty places are more liable to destruction
than those who dwell by the rivers or on the sea-shore; and from this
calamity the Nile, who is our never failing saviour, saves and delivers
us. When, on the other hand, the gods purge the earth with a deluge
of water, among you herdsmen and shepherds on the mountains are
the survivors, whereas those of you who live in cities are carried by
the rivers into the sea: but in this country neither at that time nor any
other does the water come from above on the fields, having always
a tendency to come up from below, for which reason the things
perceived here are said to be the oldest. The fact is that wherever the
extremity of winter frost or of summer sun does not prevent, the
human race is always increasing at times, and at others diminishing
in numbers. And whatever happened either in your country or in ours,
or in any other region of which we are informed – if any action which
is noble or great, or in any other way remarkable has taken place,
all that has been written down of old, and is preserved in our temples;
whereas you and other nations are just being provided with letters and
other things which States require; and then, at the usual period, the
stream from heaven descends like a pestilence, and leaves only those
of you who are destitute of letters and education; and thus you have
to begin all over again as children, and know nothing of what
happened in ancient times, either among us or among yourselves. As
for those genealogies of yours, which you have recounted to us, Solon,
they are no better than the tales of children; for, in the first place,
you remember one deluge only, whereas there were many of them;
and, in the next place, you do not know that there dwelt in your land
the fairest and noblest race of men which ever lived, of whom you
and your whole city are but a seed or remnant. And this was unknown
to you because for many generations the survivors of that destruction
died and made no sign. For there was a time, Solon, before that great
deluge of all, when the city which is now Athens was first in war,
and was preeminent for the excellence of her laws, and is said to have
performed the noblest deeds, and to have had the fairest constitution
of any of which tradition tells us, under the face of heaven.'[6]

Being highly curious about these former citizens, Solon then
questioned the priest as to who they were and from whence they

came. His host, it seems, was only too happy to impart the information:

> . . .both for the sake of the goddess who is the common patron and protector and educator of both our cities. She founded your city a thousand years before ours, receiving from the Earth and Hephaestus the seed of your race, and then she founded ours, the constitution of which is set down in our sacred registers as 8,000 years old. [7]

The priest then went on to describe the system of government, laws and various classes of society that existed in the first Athens, that had been bestowed on the people by 'the goddess who was a lover of both war and wisdom' (Athene). Mention is then made of a time when:

> A power came forth out of the Atlantic Ocean, for in those times the Atlantic was navigable; and there was an island situated in front of the straits which you call the Columns of Heracles (Hercules): the island was larger than Libya and Asia put together, and was the way to other islands, and from the islands you might pass through the whole of the opposite continent which surrounded the true ocean; for this sea which is within the straits of Heracles is only a harbour, having a narrow entrance, but that other is a real sea, and the surrounding land may be most truly called a continent. Now in the island of Atlantis there was a great and wonderful empire, which had rule over the whole island and several others, as well as over parts of the continent; and, besides these, they subjected the parts of Libya within the columns of Heracles as far as Egypt, and of Europe as far as Tyrrhenia. [8]

I cannot read these passages without experiencing an uncanny feeling that they are prophetic, and that many of the events described therein could apply just as much to our world today. No doubt Gaia does see fit to cull her hominid population from time to time, just as we, in turn, apply similar restrictions to many of the other life-forms with which we share the generosity of her bosom. I am sure that by the end of this book many a reader may also feel, as I do, that the Egyptian priests and the Greek sages were correct in their assessment of the regular periodicity of axis tilt and pole shifts. After all, taking into account Gaia's own age, it is only comparatively recently that hominids have made their appearance here and like the dinosaurs we may be totally expendable to her and the continuation of our species a hindrance to her own evolution. Only time will tell. Perhaps our examination of the events that led up to the fall of the Atlantean empire might help us to avoid a similar plight, as the myths consistently inform us that such major catastrophes are inevitably visited upon us by the 'gods' as a punishment for the evil ways into which we have fallen. (In metaphysical language, the disregard of basic cosmic laws.)

But to return to our narrative, subsequent studies have shown there to be two distinct periods of Greek (and Egyptian) history exposed here. According to the *Oera Linda Book*, a work of great antiquity that contains the annals of the ancient Frisians, an antediluvian maritime people whose country was called Atland(?), when their lands, which adjoined the western coastline of Scandinavia, broke up and sank following a drastic change in the earth's axial rotation, those Frisians that escaped intermarried with other northern European people and set about colonizing several areas of the Mediterranean and North Africa. Nor is this account of their ancient habitat a mere myth: borings taken in that precise area of the North Sea in the late 1980s showed that the sea-bed in those parts had been above land approximately *seven thousand years earlier* – *c.*5000 BC! Now the Frisians were a matriarchal society, led by female warriors. Both the Egyptian Neith and the Greek Athene are thus depicted, while both goddesses shared another attribute – the weaver's shuttle. The tale told to Solon by the Egyptian priests could therefore be seen to receive verification from two sources: geology and the myths of another land.

The *Oera Linda Book* also tells of how their warrior priestess, Min-Erva, at the head of a group of her people, landed on the shores of prehistoric Greece and founded the first Athens.* The Frisians taught the local people many of the arts of civilization which they, in turn, had probably learned from the Atlanteans. However, in spite of the fact that they adhered to strong metaphysical beliefs and practices (who didn't in those days!) they were basically monotheistic, so when the time came for their Frisian warrior queen to depart this world, the local people sought to deify her and erect a statue in her honour, which they did,

* The Frisian influence is believed by some authorities to be evidenced in the names of places and people that bear the prefix 'Min'. The Roman goddess Minerva, equated by scholars, and the Romans themselves, with the Greek Athene, was adapted from an Etruscan divinity of similar sounding name whose origin is also shrouded in the mists of antiquity.

depicting her in the full armour she had worn upon her arrival. Protest as they may, the remaining Frisians were unable to hold out against the newly acquired religious fervour of the Hellenes. Shortly after that the old Athens was reduced to rubble by earth tremors and other elemental disturbances, which changed the land from a moist and verdant terrain to the hot, dry country of later years. The picture of their much loved protectress had, however, subconsciously lingered in the hearts of the people, to resurface centuries later when their city was finally rebuilt. Then, in the persona of the goddess Athene, she was pronounced tutelary deity of the Greek capital which carries her name to this day.

Like the ruling caste of ancient Atlantis, the Frisians were an exceptionally tall, fair-haired, blue-eyed people. Egyptian history evidences the arrival of a group of people known as the *Shemsu-Hor*, translated as The Followers (or Children) of Horus, of whom Professor Emery writes:

> . . . towards the close of the fourth millennium BC we find the people known traditionally as the 'Followers of Horus' apparently forming a civilized aristocracy or master race ruling over the whole of Egypt. The theory of the existence of this master race is supported by the discovery that graves of the late predynastic period in the northern part of Upper Egypt were found to contain the anatomical remains of a people whose skulls are of greater size and whose bodies were larger than those of the natives, the difference being so marked that any suggestion that these people derived from the earlier stock is impossible. The fusion of the two races must have been considerable, but it was not so rapid that by the time of the Unification it could be considered in any way accomplished, for throughout the whole of the Archaic Period the distinction between the civilized aristocracy and the mass of the natives is very marked, particularly in regard to their burial customs. Only with the close of the Second Dynasty do we find evidence of the lower orders adopting the funerary architecture and mode of burial of their masters.
>
> The racial origin of these invaders is not known and the route they took in their penetration of Egypt is equally obscure. [9]

Professor Emery assures us that these conquering aristocrats came in strange vessels with a high prow, totally dissimilar to anything used by the Egyptians at that time. Emery sees the hint of a Mesopotamian influence in these craft, but they strike me as being more typically Norse, although I confess to being no expert in such matters. The arrival of the Shemsu-Hor is depicted in the Gebel-el-Arak knife handle, which has been dated to the archaic period.

Figure 8. The Gebel-el-Arak knife-handle. Note the strange prows on the ship, which surely suggest a Frisian rather than Mesopotamian origin?

R. A. Schwaller de Lubicz, the Alsatian scholar and expert in Egyptian antiquities, says of the Shemsu-Hor:

> The term *Shemsu-Hor*, incorrectly translated as 'Companions of Horus, literally means *Followers of Horus* in the precise sense of 'those who follow the Path of Horus', that is, the 'Horian Way', also called the solar way or *Paths of Ra*. This epithet applies to superior beings who produced the race of Pharaohs, as opposed to the majority of people who followed the common way, the way of Osiris. These *Followers of Horus* bear with them a knowledge of 'divine origin', and unify the country with it.[10]

The *Papyrus of Turin* gives a complete list of the kings who reigned over Upper and Lower Egypt from Menes to the New Empire. Unfortunately, most of the names and dates are missing, but the remaining fragments establish that nine dynasties were mentioned which, Schwaller de Lubicz tells us, were:

... the (venerables) of Memphis, the venerables of the North, and finally the *Shemsu-Hor* ...

Fortunately the last two lines have survived almost intact, as have indications regarding the number of years:

> ... venerables Shemsu-Hor, 13,429 years
> Reigns up to Shemsu-Hor, 23,200 years (total 36,620) King Menes. [11]

Diodorus Siculus quotes several earlier sources as stating that a succession of gods and heroes ruled Egypt for some 18,000 years, and these in turn were followed by mortal kings whose reigns totalled 15,000 years in all, indicating a historical span of 33,000 years. Manetho's figures differ somewhat in that he allots 15,150 years to the divinities, and 9,777 years to those kings who preceded Menes, his total amounting to 24,927 years of prehistory. Georgius Syncellus wrote of an ancient chronicle that indicated a period of 36,525 years, while Herodotus topped them all with the statement: '... they also said that during this long succession of centuries, on four separate occasions, the sun moved from his wonted course, twice rising where he now sets, and twice setting where he now rises.' [12]

Here we would appear to have confirmation of several factors: (a) the details given to Solon by the priest of Sais – that both Athens and Sais were founded by tall, fair strangers from across the seas; (b) the arrival on Egyptian shores of another group of tall, fair strangers prior to the Atlantean cataclysm, and (c) the pre-Atlantean (Mu-an) influence in archaic Egypt as affirmed by Churchward. The times given are, however, highly questionable unless we go along with Spence's idea that Atlantis did not go down in one piece but shattered slowly over a period of some 3,000 years. Solon's goddesses who founded Sais and Athens were either Frisians, or Atlanteans who had settled elsewhere and chosen to move on. Likewise the Shemsu-Hor could have been survivors from the final cataclysm, or, as is more likely, Atlantean colonists who arrived on Egyptian soil prior to the Deluge. We do know that these followers of the Way of Horus were solar rather than lunar orientated, while they appeared to acknowledge other Neters in addition to Horus (Heru) and Ra. One thing that does fascinate me about them is their wearing of ceremonial tails (see Figure 9), a privilege, it would seem, that was reserved for the higher echelons of their race. That they were fair and blue-eyed may be

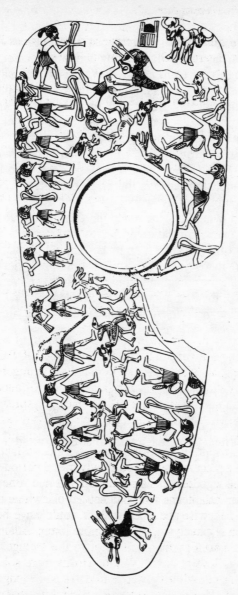

Figure 9. So-called Prehistoric Palette found at Hierakonpolis, one fragment of which is in the Louvre and two others in the British Museum. Note the Ritual Tails: did these carry some Atlantean significance?

evidenced in the fact that during the ensuing years, amulets of the 'Eye of Horus' were inevitably shown with a blue eye, while the *Book of the Dead* states '. . . Horus of the blue eyes cometh unto you.'[13] And finally, (d) Herodotus's reference to the changing positions of the sun, which surely refers to former axis tilts.

According to the *Oera Linda Book* the ancient matrist Frisians were monotheists, their supreme deity. Wr'alda, (lit. trans. 'Old Ancient', or 'Oldest Being') representing the unchangeable, perfect, almighty essence, which appeared to incorporate both genders in balanced proportion. Wr'alda's creation, however, was made manifest through the 'Three Mothers of Mankind', Lyda, Finda and Frya, (The Triple Goddess?) who are described as having founded the black, yellow and white races respectively, and who were subsequently worshipped by ensuing generations of Frisians following the Tilt. Since the *Oera Linda Book* doubtless underwent many translations prior to its present form, however, I do not feel that too much emphasis should be placed on actual names, as many of these were doubtless added later to accommodate the prevailing climates of social and religious belief. For example, the date given for the inundation of Atland – 2193 BC – has now been proven geologically to be inaccurate, the subsidence having taken place several thousand years earlier, around 5000 BC, as previously discussed.

Isis and Osiris (Auset and Ausar to the Egyptians) are believed to have arrived on Egyptian soil 12,452 years ago, which according to the Turin Papyrus would place them in the period of the Shemsu-Hor. In fact this date, which represents the equivalent of our 1990, is still observed by the Ammonites, an Egyptian people who claim direct descent from the pharaohs of old, and who have kept the ancient ways and religion alive to this very day. This figure subtracted from 1990 gives us 10462 BC, which equates with the period given to Solon by the Egyptian priests as the time when the main island of Atlantis sank. On the other hand, as we shall see, there is an equal amount of evidence to suggest that it was around 10462 BC that Isis, Osiris and Thoth arrived in Egypt, probably as part of a colonizing expedition. The mystery deepens, or does it?

Endnotes
1. Churchward, J. *The Lost Continent of Mu*, p.63.
2. Ibid. p.68.
3. Hope, M. *Atlantis: Myth or Reality?* pp.105–8.

4. Spence, L. *The History of Atlantis*, p.64.
5. Taylor, S. (ed.). *Atlantis, Past and to Come*, pp.20–21.
6. Donnelly, I. *Atlantis: The Antediluvian World*, pp.7–21.
7. Ibid. pp.7–21.
8. Ibid. pp.7–21.
9. Emery, W. B. *Archaic Egypt*, pp.39–40.
10. Schwaller de Lubicz, R.A. *Sacred Science*, p.111.
11. Ibid. p.86.
12. Ibid. p.87.
13. Budge, E.A. Wallis. *The Book of the Dead*, Vol.3, p.602.

3. PLATO'S ATLANTEANS

Since many scholars are of the opinion that the story told to Solon
by his Egyptian host concerning those enigmatic visitors, who
under the leadership of their goddess Athene/Neith founded the
cities of Athens and Sais respectively, does not relate to Atlantis
or the Atlantean people as such, who, then, were those Atlanteans
that Plato was to record for posterity? As we have already
discussed, two different periods of prehistory would appear to be
involved here, both of which became confused with the passage
of time as they eventually degenerated into myth and legend. It
should also be borne in mind that Critias the younger was only
ten years old when he first heard the tale, and the points likely
to interest a boy of that age might not necessarily be those that
would excite later scholars. Besides, by the time the story came
to the ears of Plato it had probably acquired a degree of
embroidery, as may be evidenced in the Hellenized names and
insistence upon emphasizing the military prowess of the Hellenic
ancestry. Assuming, however, that there is some vestige of truth
to be found in this strange tale, a closer look at Plato's narration
which gives a fairly detailed description of the island continent,
its founder god, the lifestyle of its peoples, its cities, sciences,
commerce and so forth, might serve to help the reader effect the
necessary distinctions between Atlantean fact and Greek fiction.

Plato's Island Continent
The constant allusion to familiar Greek names is guaranteed to
provoke incredulity among the more sceptical, although Plato

justly hastens to assure his readers that these are inserted purely for convenience, the original nomenclatures having been long since forgotten. According to Greek mythology the brothers Zeus, Poseidon, and Hades were allotted dominion over the sky, oceans and chthonic regions respectively, and Plato assures us that it was to Poseidon, as god of the Sea, that rulership over the island continent of Atlantis therefore fell. Having thus established his throne, Poseidon duly begat children by a mortal woman, and this part-human/part-divine 'family' settled in what was obviously seen as the best part of the island. The Atlantean dynasty had commenced. Plato takes up the tale:

On the side towards the sea, and in the centre of the whole island, there was a plain which is said to have been the fairest of all plains and very fertile. Near the plain again, and also in the centre of the island, at a distance of about fifty stadia* there was a mountain, not very high on any side. In this mountain there dwelt one of the earth-born primeval men of that country,** whose name was Evenor, and he had a wife named Leucippe, and they had an only daughter, whose name was Cleito. The maiden was growing up to womanhood when her father and mother died. Poseidon fell in love with her, and had intercourse with her; and, in breaking the ground, enclosed the hill in which she dwelt all round, making alternate zones of sea and land, larger and smaller, encircling one another; there were two of land and three of water, which he turned as with a lathe out of the centre of the island, equidistant every way, so that no man could get to the island, for ships and voyages were not yet heard of. He himself, as he was a god, found no difficulty in making special arrangements for the centre island, bringing two streams of water under the earth, which he caused to ascend as springs, one of warm water and one of cold, and making every variety of food to spring up abundantly in the earth. He also begat and brought up five pairs of male children, dividing the island of Atlantis into ten portions; he gave to the first-born of the eldest pair his mother's dwelling and the surrounding allotment, which was the largest and best, and made him king over the rest; the others he made princes, and gave them rule over many men and a large territory. And he named them all: the eldest, who was king, he named Atlas, and from him the whole island and ocean

---

* It is generally believed that a stadium was 607 feet in length (185 meters), so 50 stadia would be 5.75 miles (9 kilometres), 3,000 stadia would equal 344.89 miles (555 kilometres), and so forth.
** Are we to deduce from this that there were aboriginals on the lands settled by the evolved Atlanteans?

received the name Atlantic. To his twin-brother, who was born after him and obtained as his lot the extremity of the island toward the pillars of Heracles, as far as the country which is still called the region of Gades in that part of the world, he gave the name which in the Hellenic language is Eumelus, in the language of the country which is named after him Gadierus [Cadiz]. Of the second pair of twins he called one Ampheres and the other Evaemon. To the third pair of twins he gave the name Mneseus to the elder and Autochthon to the one who followed him. Of the fourth pair of twins he called the elder Elasippus and the younger Mestor. And of the fifth pair he gave to the elder the name of Azaes, and to the younger Diaprepes. All these and their descendants were the inhabitants and rulers of divers islands in the open sea: and also, as has been already said, they held sway in the other direction over the country within the Pillars as far as Egypt and Tyrrhenia. Now Atlas had a numerous and honourable family, and his eldest branch always retained the kingdom, which the eldest son handed on to his eldest for many generations, and they had such an amount of wealth as was never before possessed by kings and potentates, and is not likely ever to be again, and they were furnished with everything which they could have, both in city and country. For, because of the greatness of their empire, many things were brought to them from foreign countries, and the island itself provided much of what was required by them for the uses of life. In the first place they dug out of the earth whatever was to be found there, mineral as well as metal, and that which is now only a name, and was then something more than a name – orichalcum – was dug out of the earth in many parts of the island, and, with the exception of gold, was esteemed the most precious of metals among the men of those days. There was an abundance of wood for carpenters' work, and sufficient maintenance for tame and wild animals. Moreover, there were a great number of elephants in the island, and there was a provision for animals of every kind, both for those which live in lakes and marshes and rivers, and also for those which live in mountains and on plains, and therefore for the animal which is the largest and most voracious of them. Also, whatever fragrant things there are in the earth, whether roots, or herbage, or woods, or distilling drops of flowers or fruits, grew and thrived in that land; and again, the cultivated fruit of the earth, both the dry edible fruit and other species of food, which we call by the name of legumes, and the fruits having a hard rind, affording drinks, and meats, and ointments, and good store of chestnuts and the like, which may be used to play with, and are fruits which spoil with keeping – and the pleasant kind of dessert which console us after dinner, when we are full and tired of eating – all these that sacred island lying beneath the sun brought fair and wondrous in infinite abundance. All these things they received from the earth, and they employed themselves in constructing their temples, and palaces, and harbors, and docks; and they arranged the whole country in the following manner:

First of all they bridged over the zones of sea which surrounded the ancient metropolis, and made a passage into and out of the royal palace; and then they began to build the palace in the habitation of the god and of their ancestors. This they continued to ornament in successive generations, every king surpassing the one who came before him to the utmost of his power, until they made the building a marvel to behold for size and for beauty. And, beginning from the sea, they dug a canal three hundred feet in width and one hundred feet in depth, and fifty stadia in length, which they carried through to the outermost zone, making a passage from the sea up to this, which became a harbor, and leaving an opening sufficient to enable the largest vessels to find ingress. Moreover they divided the zones of land which parted the zones of sea, constructing bridges of such width as would leave a passage for a single trireme to pass out of one into another, and roofed them over; and there was a way underneath for the ships, for the banks of the zones were raised considerably above the water. Now the largest of the zones into which a passage was cut from the sea was three stadia in breadth, and the zone of land which came next of equal breadth; but the next two, as well the zone of water as of land, were two stadia, and the one which surrounded the central island was a stadium only in width. The island in which the palace was situated had a diameter of five stadia. This, and the zones and the bridge, which was the sixth part of a stadium in width, they surrounded by a stone wall, on either side placing towers, and gates on the bridges where the sea passed in. The stone which was used in the work they quarried from underneath the centre island and from underneath the zones, on the outer, as well as the inner side. One kind of stone was white, another black, and the third red; and, as they quarried they at the same time hollowed out docks double within, having roofs formed out of the native rock. Some of their buildings were simple, but in others they put together different stones, which they intermingled for the sake of ornament, to be a natural source of delight. The entire circuit of the wall which went round the outermost one they covered with a coating of brass, and the circuit of the next wall they coated with tin, and the third, which encompassed the citadel, flashed with the red light of orichalcum. The palaces in the interior of the citadel were constructed in this wise: In the centre was a holy temple dedicated to Cleito and Poseidon, which remained inaccessible, and was surrounded by an enclosure of gold; this was the spot in which they originally begat the race of the ten princes, and thither they annually brought the fruits of the earth in their season from all the ten portions, and performed sacrifices to each of them. Here, too, was Poseidon's own temple, of a stadium in length and half a stadium in width, and of a proportionate height, having a sort of barbaric splendor. All the outside of the temple, with the exception of the pinnacles, they covered with silver, and the pinnacles with gold. In the interior of the temple the roof was of ivory, adorned everywhere with gold and silver and orichalcum; all the other parts of the walls and pillars and floor they lined with orichalcum. In the temple they placed statues of gold: there was the god himself standing in a chariot – the charioteer of six winged horses – and of such a size that he touched the roof of the building with his head; around him there were a hundred Nereids riding on dolphins, for such was thought to be the number of them in that day. There were also in the interior of the temple other images which had been dedicated by private individuals. And around the temple on the outside were placed statues of gold of all the ten kings and of their wives; and there were many other great offerings, both of kings and of private individuals, coming both from the city itself and the foreign cities over which they held sway. There was an altar, too, which in size and workmanship corresponded to the rest of the work, and there were palaces in like manner which answered to the greatness of the kingdom and the glory of the temple.

In the next place, they used fountains both of cold and hot springs; these were very abundant, and both kinds wonderfully adapted to use by reason of the sweetness and excellence of their waters. They constructed buildings about them, and planted suitable trees; also cisterns, some open to the heaven, others which they roofed over, to be used in winter as warm baths. There were the king's baths, and the baths of private persons, which were kept apart; also separate baths for women, and others again for horses and cattle, and to them they gave as much adornment as was suitable for them. The water which ran off they carried, some to the grove of Poseidon, where were growing all manner of trees of wonderful height and beauty, owing to the excellence of the soil; the remainder was conveyed by aqueducts which passed over the bridges to the outer circles: and there were many temples built and dedicated to many gods; also gardens and places of exercise, some for men, and some set apart for horses, in both of the two islands formed by the zones; and in the centre of the larger of the two there was a race-course of a stadium in width, and in length allowed to extend all round the island, for horses to race in. Also there were guard-houses at intervals for the body-guard, the more trusted of whom had their duties appointed to them in the lesser zone, which was nearer the Acropolis; while the most trusted of all had houses given them within the citadel, and about the persons of the kings. The docks were full of triremes and naval stores, and all things were quite ready for use. Enough of the plan of the royal palace.

Crossing the outer harbors, which were three in number, you would come to a wall which began at the sea and went all round: this was everywhere distant fifty stadia from the largest zone and harbor, and enclosed the whole, meeting at the mouth of the channel toward the sea. The entire area was densely crowded with habitations; and the canal and the largest of the harbors were full of vessels and merchants coming from all parts, who, from their numbers, kept up a multitudinous sound of human voices and din of all sorts night and day. I have repeated his descriptions of the city and the parts about the ancient palace nearly as he gave them, and now I must endeavor to describe the nature and arrangement of the rest of the country.

The whole country was described as being very lofty and precipitous on the side of the sea, but the country immediately about and surrounding the city was a level plain, itself surrounded by mountains which descended toward the sea; it was smooth and even, but of an oblong shape extending in one direction three thousand stadia, and going up the country from the sea through the centre of the island two thousand stadia; the whole region of the island lies toward the south, and is sheltered from the north. The surrounding mountains he celebrated for their number and size and beauty, in which they exceeded all that are now to be seen anywhere; having in them also many wealthy inhabited villages, and rivers and lakes, and meadows supplying food enough for every animal, wild or tame, and wood of various sorts, abundant for every kind of work. I will now describe the plain, which had been cultivated during many ages by many generations of kings. It was rectangular, and for the most part straight and oblong; and what it wanted of the straight line followed the line of the circular ditch. The depth and width and length of this ditch were incredible, and gave the impression that such a work, in addition to so many other works, could hardly have been wrought to the hand of man. But I must say what I have heard. It was excavated to the depth of a hundred feet, and its breadth was a stadium everywhere; it was carried round the whole of the plain, and was ten thousand stadia in length. It received the streams which came down from the mountains, and winding round the plain, and touching the city at various points, was there let off into the sea. From above, likewise, straight canals of a hundred feet in width were cut in the plain, and again let off into the ditch, toward the sea; these canals were at intervals of a hundred stadia, and by them they brought down the wood from the mountains to the city, and conveyed the fruits of the earth in ships, cutting transverse passages from one canal into another, and to the city. Twice in the year they gathered the fruits of the earth – in winter having the benefit of the rains, and in summer introducing the water of the canals. As to the population, each of the lots in the plain had an appointed chief of men who were fit for military service, and the size of the lot was to be a square of ten stadia each way, and the total number of all the lots was sixty thousand.

And of the inhabitants of the mountains and of the rest of the country there was also a vast multitude having leaders, to whom they were assigned according to their dwellings and villages. The leader was required to furnish for the war the sixth portion of a war-chariot, so as to make up a total of ten thousand chariots; also two horses and riders upon them, and a light chariot without a seat, accompanied by a fighting man on foot carrying a small shield, and having a charioteer mounted to guide the horses; also, he was bound to furnish two heavy-armed men, two archers, two slingers, three stone-shooters, and three javelin men, who were skirmishers, and four sailors to make up a complement of twelve hundred ships. Such was the order of war in the royal city – that of the other nine governments was different in each of them, and would be wearisome to narrate. As to offices and honors, the following was the arrangement from the first; Each of the ten kings, in his own division and in his own city, had the absolute control of the citizens, and in many cases of the laws, punishing and slaying whomsoever he would.

Now the relations of their governments to one another were regulated by the injunctions of Poseidon as the law had handed them down. These were inscribed by the first men on a column of orichalcum, which was situated in the middle of the island, at the temple of Poseidon, whither the people were gathered together every fifth and sixth years alternately, thus giving equal honor to the odd and to the even number. And when they were gathered together they consulted about public affairs, and inquired if any one had transgressed in anything, and passed judgment on him accordingly – and before they passed judgment they gave their pledges to one another in this wise: There were bulls who had the range of the temple of Poseidon; and the ten who were left alone in the temple, after they had offered prayers to the gods that they might take the sacrifices which were acceptable to them, hunted the bulls without weapons, but with staves and nooses; and the bull which they caught they led up to the column; the victim was then struck on the head by them, and slain over the sacred inscription. Now on the column, besides the law, there was inscribed an oath invoking mighty curses on the disobedient. When, therefore, after offering sacrifice according to their customs, they had burnt the limbs of the bull, they mingled a cup and cast a clot of blood for each of them; the rest of the victim they took to the fire, after having made a purification of the column all round. Then they drew from the cup in golden vessels, and, pouring a libation on the fire, they swore that they would judge according to the laws on the column, and would punish any one who had previously transgressed, and that for the future they would not, if they could help, transgress any of the inscriptions, and would not command or obey any ruler who commanded them to act otherwise than according to the laws of their father Poseidon. This was the prayer which each of them offered up for himself and for his family, at the same time drinking, and dedicating the vessel in the temple of the god; and, after spending some necessary time at supper, when darkness came on and the fire about the sacrifice was cool, all of them put on most beautiful azure robes, and, sitting on the ground at night near the embers of the sacrifices on which they had sworn, and extinguishing all the fire about the temple, they received and gave judgment, if any of them had any accusation to bring against any one; and, when they had given judgment, at daybreak they wrote down their sentences on a golden tablet, and deposited them as memorials with their robes. There were many special laws which the several kings had inscribed about the temples, but the most important was the following: That they were not to take up arms against one another, and they were all to come to the rescue if any one in any city attempted to overthrow the royal house. Like their ancestors, they were to deliberate in common about war and other matters, giving the supremacy to the family of Atlas; and the king was not to have the power of life and death over any of his kinsmen, unless he had the assent of the majority of the ten kings.

Such was the vast power which the god settled in the lost island of Atlantis; and this he afterward directed against our land on the following pretext, as traditions tell: For many generations, as long as the divine nature lasted in them, they were obedient to the laws, and well-affectioned toward the gods, who were their kinsmen; for they possessed true and in every way great spirits, practising gentleness and wisdom in the various chances of life, and in their intercourse with one another. They despised everything but virtue, not caring for their present state of life, and thinking lightly on the possession of gold and other property, which seemed only a burden to them; neither were they intoxicated by luxury; nor did wealth deprive them of their self-control; but they were sober, and saw clearly that all these goods are increased by virtuous friendship with one another, and that by excessive zeal for them, and honor of them, the good of them is lost, and friendship perishes with them.

By such reflections, and by the continuance in them of a divine nature, all that which we have described waxed and increased in them; but when this divine portion began to fade away in them, and became diluted too often, and with too much of the mortal admixture, and the human nature got the upper-hand, then, they being unable to bear their fortune, became unseemly, and to him who had an eye to see, they began to appear base, and had lost the fairest of their precious gifts; but to those who had no eye to see the true happiness, they still appeared glorious and blessed at the very time when they were filled with unrighteous avarice and power. Zeus, the god of gods, who rules with law, and is able to see into such things, perceiving that an honorable race was in a most wretched state, and wanting to inflict punishment on them, that they might be chastened and improved, collected all the gods into his most holy habitation, which, being placed in the centre of the world, sees all things that partake of generation. And when he had called them together he spake as follows: . . .[1]

[Here Plato's story abruptly ends.]

From this text we may assume that the Atlantis to which Plato was referring was that of the latter days, although the obvious nepotism suggests that the kingly pattern had probably been set during the Age of Leo. Lewis Spence sees the Bull cults as having Cro Magnon connections, the bull being one of the totem animals much represented in Aurignacian cave art. They also have a distinctly Minoan flavour about them, but then Minoa might well have inherited them from the Atlantean originals, although it is worth bearing in mind that this may be another of those historical confusions between the Atlanteans and those sea-peoples who later made a nuisance of themselves in many areas of the Mediterranean. Besides, Bull cults surely belong with the Taurean Age. On the other hand, some of the details are correct; the blue garments that were the hallmark of the Atlantean priesthood, for example, so perhaps these unwholesome sacrifices were linked to the degeneracy that set in during the latter days.

What I do not doubt is the very graphic description of the capital city and its system of canals, harbours, palaces and temples. So deeply must this particular design have been imprinted on the collective unconscious of mankind that it is repeated with regularity in prehistoric stone circles and altars. Of course it could be argued that the Atlanteans adopted it from the Mu-ans, but were this to have been the case, then they must at least be credited for refining it and becoming aware of its cosmic significance. My own feeling is that it carries extraterrestrial connotations, and is therefore not the exclusive property of any earthly culture or creed.

Whichever stance we may choose to adopt over Plato's narrative, taking into account the history of his time and the culture in which he and his contemporaries lived, Plato himself, Critias the Younger, and the other sources from Solon downwards, were obviously describing a technically advanced and highly sophisticated civilization, the likes of which none of them had ever experienced or read about in the history that was available to them at that time. One cannot help but feel sad that such a wonderful race, that appeared to enjoy so many blessings, saw fit to end up abusing both its spiritual and temporal powers.

The fact that things were not always that way, however, may be evidenced in Plato's reference to the many earlier generations that were content to live within the order of divine (cosmic?) law, despising the materialism of the world and seeking only virtue. These people, he tells us, were kinsmen of the gods, whom we would probably equate with those offsprings that resulted from the Biblical accounts of couplings between 'the sons of God and the daughters of men'. There is, however, a strong genetic intimation here, since Plato insists that it was the dilution of the divine gene that led to their eventual downfall. Which raises the following points: a) Is there such a thing as a 'divine gene' that could be seen in the light of currently favoured metaphysical theories as having resulted from an interbreeding between an alien species and an early development of *Homo sapiens*, and b) does this gene imbibe its carriers with a kind of spirituality, or virtuous sensitivity, that renders them vulnerable to the rougher, more materialistic element in society which metaphysicians would see in terms of youthful soul-age or cosmic immaturity? In the light of the fact that many doctors and psychologists now acknowledge that the soma reflects the psyche, Plato's explanation is not so easily dismissed. From what Plato tells us, plus what some of us are able to 'recall' of life in Atlantis in the distant past, it would seem that while the island continent was ruled by a gentle, spiritually motivated priesthood, who cared for the needs of its people, observed cosmic law, applied its extensive scientific knowledge to the good of society at large, and acknowledged its divine ancestry or cosmic origins, all went well. But as the knowledge of this Garden of Eden spread to other parts of the world, many less scrupulous people homed in on it. These outsiders eventually interbred with the native Atlanteans, and the 'divine gene' became so diluted that the original programme it carried was soon forgotten.

So what was this gene and who were its progenitors? Now one can adopt any of several approaches to the E.T. question, Professor Hoyle's 'panspermia theory', for example, which conceives of alien microorganisms distributed throughout interstellar space, and penetrating the Earth's atmosphere. This concept is not entirely new, however, as Hoyle tells us:

It was considered already during the 19th century, in particular by British physicist Lord Kelvin. Unfortunately, however, the possibility of understanding biological evolution here on Earth in terms of this concept was not appreciated, with the consequence that scientists became forced away from what is almost surely the correct theory by the rising tide of Darwinism. This was in spite of a valiant effort early in the present century by the Swedish chemist Svante Arrhenius to support the 'panspermia' theory (meaning 'seeds everywhere') by carefully reasoned arguments.[7]

Alternative ideas include beings from the Sirius system descending to Earth for a sufficient period to enable them to bestow their highly evolved gene on 'the daughters of men' either via the normal channels of intercourse or, as some like to believe, by genetic engineering. If we think of the latter in terms of our present work in this field, then the mind does boggle. But taking into account that these beings, whoever they were (assuming there were such creatures) were probably centuries further advanced than we are today, it could have involved a process as simple as partaking of a glass of delicious liquid, breathing the essence of a strange flower, or simply the voluntary act of *seeking enlightenment*. The pros and cons of any of these arguments do not concern me, however, since the Genome Project – a proposed survey of the peoples of the Earth, based on analysis of their personal, genetic code – should resolve the question once and for all. A forerunner is genetic fingerprinting, which identifies individuals by their DNA. I am inclined to believe that such a gene still exists, and that its carriers are easily identified by certain physical, psychological and spiritual traits. But more of that later.

The thing that has puzzled scholars and metaphysicians alike down the centuries is Plato's abrupt ending to this otherwise intriguing and exciting narrative. What *was* it that Zeus said? And why this unfinished ending, which is totally out of keeping with Plato's other works? Various suggestions have been offered, but my own feeling is that Plato did finish it, but someone *removed it later, for religious or political reasons*. Those words of admonition from 'on high' obviously struck home with *someone* somewhere among the sands of time, and that 'someone' must have held a position of power sufficient to enable him to obliterate the text of a scholar of the magnitude of Plato. Perhaps we shall never know, but of this I am convinced – were we to have that original text before us to read today, *the warning would apply as strongly as it did to the peoples of latter-day Atlantis*.

Endnotes
1. Donnelly, I. *Atlantis: The Antediluvian World*, pp.7–21.
2. Hoyle, F. *The Intelligent Universe*, p.158.

4. ATLANTIS – WHEN AND WHERE?

Over the years researchers have come up with several ideas regarding where the fabled island of Atlantis was actually located. Before we settle for Plato's Atlantic island continent, consideration should be given to the pros and cons of alternative sites.

Thera (Santorini)
In the late 1960s Thera, an island in the Greek Cyclydes north of Crete, was the subject of much publicity as a possible site for the Old Country. Professor A. G. Galanopoulos, an archaeologist and seismologist, and archaeologist Dr Spiridon Marinatos, were convinced that this tiny island, which was badly shaken by a volcanic eruption around 1500–1400 BC, bore many similarities to Plato's legendary continent. Little is left of the original Thera, but even if the island had been much larger originally, it hardly tallies with the dimensions given by Plato, and the dates involved certainly do not coincide. I do not doubt that a flourishing culture once held court on the old Thera which, from the dates implied, would appear to have more in common with the Minoan or Mycenaean cultures. A more detailed apology for my dismissal of this and other suggested Atlantean sites is to be found in *Atlantis: Myth or Reality?*.

Tartessos, Southern Spain – Northern Morocco
Tartessos – the Biblical Tharshish – once housed a trading nation whose fleets supplied luxury goods to kings and potentates, most

notably King Solomon. Herodotus (fifth century BC) tells of a great city called Tartessos, beyond the Pillars of Hercules, which mysteriously disappeared, due, perhaps, to some natural catastrophe, or subsequent conquest by the Carthaginians. But could this have been Atlantis itself? I think not.

Tunisia
The salt lake Schott el Hammeina was believed by some researchers to be the locality known in earlier times as the Lake of Atlantes or Lake Tritonis, thus associating it with the legend of Triton, son of Poseidon and Amphitrite. Some of the ruins investigated, however, turned out to be of Roman origin, so any name association probably derived from Graeco-Roman sources. Once again, the dimensions and other features hardly accord with Plato's account.

West and East Africa
While there would appear to be some vague mythological and ancient religious associations which connect Yorubaland and other sites along the Nigerian coast with Atlantis, these could also be seen in the Mu-an context on the one hand, or they could be due to trading that took place between the latter day Atlanteans and the African peoples on the other. Besides, there is no evidence in these areas of the kind of catastrophe that is believed to have overtaken the Old Country.

The Americas
America would seem to be an obvious choice for Plato's 'opposite continent' that was believed to exist beyond Atlantis, and to have once been approachable from the Old Country via a series of islands that subsequently sank. However, although the ocean has reclaimed large tracts of the eastern seaboard, the Americas can hardly be described as 'sunken', while there would appear to be little if any evidence of the kind of catastrophe that is believed to have afflicted Atlantis in its latter days.

Yucatan and Central America
Similarities between Mayan art forms, culture and science and those of ancient Egypt have led many scholars to conclude that both nations must have drawn their inspiration from a single source – Atlantis. However, having established Mu-an connections on both sides of the Atlantic the same could also be

said of that sunken land. My own feeling is that both Mu and Atlantis left their signatures on Egyptian and Mayan culture. I recently effected a study of blood groups worldwide, which provided me with a degree of insight into the Atlantis/Mu enigma. Members of the South and Central American ruling classes certainly appear to have visited Atlantis, while their ancestors, no doubt, originally hailed from Mu.

Tiahuanaco, Bolivia, and Brazil

In spite of the evidence of lost cities in the jungle and other tales of mystery concerning places like Tiahuanaco, I see these as predominantly Mu-an, although one cannot, of course, dismiss the possibility that visiting Atlanteans may have investigated them centuries later.

Antarctica

The fact that Antarctica was once a temperate and verdant land, fully navigable, may be evidenced in the ancient maps as presented and analyzed by Professor Hapgood in his book *Maps of the Ancient Sea Kings*. Since I am in agreement with Hapgood as regards the shifting of the poles there is no reason why Antarctica could not have housed a flourishing maritime civilization at some point in its history. No doubt following the next axis tilt, which may not be as far away as many of us might hope, archaeologists will have a heyday finding the remains of a people whose shores were mapped with the kind of precision we expect from either the possession of an appropriate technology, or years of patient observation and practical research. Either way, it would seem that the Antarcticans of old, who were probably forced to flee their lands when the ice overtook them (assuming that, unlike the mammoths, they were given some warning of the impending climatic changes), made their homes elsewhere. But that, surely, constitutes the subject of another enquiry.

The Sahara Desert

The fact that during the post-glacial 'Pluvial' (the rainy period that geologists place roughly between 8000 and 4000 BC) the Sahara was a rich and verdant land has led some researchers to believe that it must have been the Atlantis described by Plato. Although the Taeuregs, like the Ammonites, have a language and tradition of great antiquity, I do not see the Sahara as a likely candidate for Atlantean soil. There is, however, a strange and interesting connection between certain fair-skinned, blue- or grey-eyed desert tribes who claim descent from 'the gods'. These 'gods' must have been a group of highly advanced and technologically-skilled beings who appeared among them and instructed them in certain matters, scant details of which have lasted in their tribal traditions to this day, although the original meanings have been long since forgotten.

The North Sea

Although many other ancient peoples are believed to have had Atlantean connections – the Etruscans, for example, whose lands in Tyrrhenia formed part of Plato's great Atlantean empire – these may be seen more in the context of later colonies than the Atlantean mainland as such, while the same could possibly be said of the North Sea. However, this area and its adjoining lands could qualify as being among the more logical sites for Atlantis since in Lurasian times the Old Country was undoubtedly attached to Greenland and parts of North America and Northern Europe. It is, therefore, little wonder that the peoples of ancient Thule, Hyperborea, and other northern territories, resembled the Atlanteans. They were probably of the same root race, and carried the A blood group and associated genetic markers that accompany the flaxen or red-haired, blue-eyed, fair or freckled skin of many Scandinavians and northern Europeans. The Atland of the Frisians is obviously one and the same as the 'Atlantis of the North' described by the German pastor and scholar Jurgen Spanuth in his erudite work. But was Atland actually Atlantis? I rather suspect that it was either an Atlantean colony, or the home of an offshoot of the white race that became isolated from the main Atlantean continent during the time of the sinking of Mu. As we shall shortly see, the two races do appear to have much in common.

The *Oera Linda Book* tells of sudden and dramatic changes of climate in those sections of their land that survived the major catastrophe that sent Atland to Davy Jones' Locker. We know from scientific sources that this inundation took place around 5000 BC, and it is also evidenced in certain archaic maps that show Antarctica as free of ice around the same period. This means that there could well be something in Richard Mooney's suggestion that although what is referred to as Würm Glaciation is estimated to have ended around 10,000 years ago, in Antarctica glaciation appears to *have commenced* some 6,000 years ago. Mooney comments:

We have theorized, from the evidence, that there was no Ice Age or Ice Ages; that, on the contrary, *the present is the period of glaciation* due to a deterioration in the earth's climate. From the evidence at hand, we can approximate a time-scale for the date of the catastrophe. The upper limit can be set at 8000 BC and the lower limit around 4000 BC. It would seem that we could narrow it down to around 6000 BC, for the first traces of settled urban communities date from that time: the oldest so far excavated are the town sites of Catal Huyuk and Jericho on the Anatolian plain in Turkey. [1]

Mooney's theories would appear to be confirmed by Professor Hapgood, who tells us:

In the last twenty years an immense quantity of research in this new field of palaeomagnetism has revealed the astonishing fact that the positions of the geographical poles have changed at least 200 times during geological history, and that no fewer than 16 of these changes took place during the last geological period, the Pleistocene Epoch.

At first it was thought that different positions of the Poles might be explained by the hypothesis of drifting continents, but it gradually became clear that while some of the various locations might be explained in this way many others could not. Geologists were forced to the conclusion that in addition to continental drift there had been displacements of the entire outer shell of the earth, the crystalline lithosphere, over the soft layers of magma below it. Such displacements would bring new areas into the polar regions. Their cause is still a matter for speculation and investigation, but it is likely that they result from the development of imbalances through the action of subcrustal currents in the magma of the earth's mantle.

In my book *The Path of the Pole*, I have given the results of this research in some detail, and have presented evidence of the occurrence of three displacements of the earth's crust in the last 100,000 years. According to my interpretation of the evidence Hudson Bay was located at the North Pole during the last ice age, and in this way I account for the ice age itself. The North American icecap, covering 4,000,000 square miles of the continent, and reflecting the sun's heat back into space, created a vast refrigerator from which cold winds blowing across the narrow North Atlantic brought about a lesser ice age in Europe, creating the Scandinavian ice sheet and many great mountain glaciers in Britain and in the mountain regions of Europe . . .

According to my interpretation of much radiocarbon and other evidence, a great shift in the earth's crust began about 17,000 years ago [15000 BC]. It was, of course, a slow movement, requiring as much as 5,000 years for its completion. North America was shifted southwards, and with it the whole western hemisphere, while the eastern hemisphere was shifted northward. The effect was to cause the melting of the great icecap in North America, while placing northern Siberia in deep freeze. This theory seems to succeed quite well in explaining not only the end of the ice age in North America and Europe but also the long standing mystery of the quantities of frozen animals that have been found in the Siberian tundra.

Antarctica was of course affected by this shift of the crust. It was moved into the Antarctic Circle. When the North Pole was in Hudson Bay the South Pole would have been located in the ocean off Wilkes Coast, and as a result most of the continent would have been ice free. The displacement of the crust would have located the pole where it is now right in the centre of the continent and brought about the vast expansion of any ice formations that might have been there before. At the same time, of course, the disappearance of the North American ice cap and the consequent warming of the Atlantic Ocean gradually melted the glaciers in Europe.[2]

While I am in agreement with Hapgood in the matter of the Pole change, from the evidence available the Siberian freeze-up would appear to have taken place rather suddenly. The stomachs of the mammoths in question have been found to contain fresh green grass, their digestive processes having obviously had no chance to cope with the contents of the stomach before the intense cold overtook them. The warming of the Atlantic Ocean following the Pole change might also appear to be at variance with Dr Otto Muck's theory that during the Atlantean period the Gulf Stream surrounded the island continent, giving it the fantastic climate it apparently enjoyed for so many years. This would of course, have held the colder weather to the north, so perhaps the two theories are not so opposed as they might seem at first glance.

Hapgood does, however, give us some facts that fall neatly into place, especially in relation to legends of the 'first Athens', which we are given to believe existed in a time when the climate of those parts was warm but moist, resulting in a lush, green terrain, totally unlike either the later Athens that witnessed the rise of the Parthenon, or the city we see today:

Following the ice age in Europe there was a climatic phase of which we find a good deal of evidence in our maps. This was a very rainy period which geologists call a 'pluvial' and which lasted for several thousand years. It was described by Edward S. Deevey, a geologist, in a symposium entitled *Climatic Change* edited by Dr Harlow Shapley, the director of the Harvard Observatory. According to

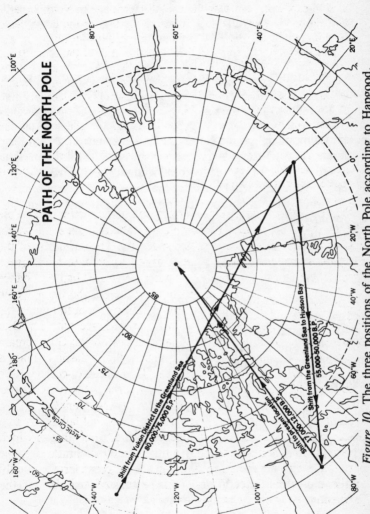

PATH OF THE NORTH POLE

Shift from Yukon District to the Greenland Sea
80,000-75,000 B.P.

Shift to present location
17,000-12,000 B.P.

Shift from the Greenland Sea to Hudson Bay
55,000-50,000 B.P.

Arctic Circle

Figure 10. The three positions of the North Pole according to Hapgood.

Deevey, who reflects the general opinion of geologists, this cold, wet period lasted until about 6,000 years ago, when it was succeeded by a period warmer and drier than now. While it lasted, the large supply of moisture resulted in more and larger rivers and lakes not only in Europe but in Africa. The Sahara Desert was then very fertile, with wide grassy plains and great forests. There were large numbers of animals of all sorts, and there was human occupation.[3]

This Pluvial indicated by Hapgood would probably have embraced the period from the latter part of the Cancerian Age through the Age of Gemini, and accounted for the many floods worldwide. There are conflicting views as to whether catastrophes of major proportions occur at the end of each Age when, according to ancient Egyptian belief, the Neter of that Age hands over the reins of rulership to the Neter who is destined to guide the Earth through the ensuing Age, or at the commencement of the next Age. Perhaps this question will be resolved in the not-too-distant future.

Dr Bruce Heezen, oceanographer with the Lamont Geographical Observatory of Columbia University, draws our attention to the fact that 11,000 years ago (9000 BC) the sea level all round the world was some 300 feet (91 metres) lower than it is today, the eastern coastline of the United States, for example, being 100 miles (161 kilometres) farther out into the Atlantic Ocean. He believes that the enormous quantities of snow and ice released at the sudden ending of the Ice Age caused the dramatic rise in sea levels world wide. But there are theories yet to be examined, not the least of which concerns the idea that there were only 360 days in the old Atlantean year, the other five, called 'epagomenal', having being acquired at the time of the tilt *which caused our planet to move ever so slightly away from the sun*. During Atlantean times, a great deal of the moisture that now constitutes part of our oceans was drawn up into the atmosphere by the solar heat, forming a protective cloud from the sun's more destructive rays. According to Mooney:

> We have assumed the earth was at this time nearer to the sun, with a consequent greater evaporation of surface water, resulting in a high-altitude water-vapour 'screen' surrounding the earth. This would have had the effect of a deeper, denser atmosphere. The surface pressure may have been slightly higher, with a consequent higher atmospheric pressure in high, mountainous regions. Another effect of this screen would have been to filter out a great deal of solar radiation, and certainly cosmic and X-radiation from extrasolar regions of the galaxy.[4]

This idea, which receives psychic confirmation in the teachings of Rudolf Steiner, is also supported by the far memories of other reliable mystics, and in the contents of some of the less hysterical channellings. A comprehensive description of the Atlantean climate will be given in a later chapter, however, when we come to discuss the history and peoples of the Old Country.

I think this is a good place to insert a table of approximate dates, which might give the reader some idea of what we do know, what science has confirmed for us, what mythology tells us, and what is still pure speculation.

Table I

35000–33000 BC Palaeolithic, or Old Stone Age (Leo or Virgo). First Can King (Churchward). Ivory Lion mask found in Hohlenstein.

32000–16000 BC Little information about Atlantis is available for this period, although the Ammonites have furnished me with an interesting list from their ancient records which will follow on after this one. The astrological Ages involved here would be those of Sagittarius, Capricorn, Aquarius, Pisces, Aries, Taurus, Gemini and Cancer.

16000–14000 BC (Age of Scorpio). The Mu-an catastrophe, changes in the Earth's crust, alteration in the position of the Poles and expansion of Ice Cap (Hapgood). Birth of Atlantean civilization?

14000–12000 BC (Age of Libra). Arrival of Auset and Ausar in Egypt in 12341 BC, according to Ammonite sources. See also Chapter 2 (and note 11) regarding the reigns of the Shemsu-Hor who, according to the Turin Papyrus, probably arrived in Egypt during this period. Similar confirmation for the antiquity of ancient Egypt is also to be found on the writings of Diodorus Siculus and Manetho (Chapter 2, note 12).

12000–10000 BC (Age of Virgo). Birth of science in Atlantis. Sacerdotal rulership prior to the reign of the Kings.

10000–8000 BC (Age of Leo). Hesiod's 'Golden Age'. Mesolithic or Middle Stone Age – commencement circa 10000 BC. Reign of the Atlantean Kings. Expansion of trade with the rest of the then civilized world. (9000 BC – sea level 300 feet lower than today (Heezen) The advent of the age of materialism and its associated moral decline. According to Plato's sources, it was around this period that Atlantis disappeared, but opinions differ as we shall shortly see.

8000–6000 BC (Age of Cancer). Hesiod's 'Silver' or Matriarchal 8Age. Neolithic, or New Stone Age – commencement circa 7000 BC. Believed by many to be the era during which Atlantis eventually sank, the Moon, as ruler of Cancer, being in some way involved in the drama. Commencement of Hapgood's 'Pluvial'.

6000–4000 BC (Age of Gemini). The sinking of Atland. Professor Emery's estimation for the arrival of the Shemsu-Hor in Egypt, although according to the Turin Papyrus the Shemsu-Hor reigned for 13,429 years *prior to* this period (see Chapter 2, notes 11 and 12).* Climatic changes – Ross Sea becomes glacial – end of Pluvial period (Hapgood).

4000–2000 BC (Age of Taurus). Bronze Age – commencement circa 3000 BC. Arrival of the 'sea people' in the Mediterranean and North African areas among others. Rise of the Minoan or Mycenaean culture with its emphasis on Bull Cults. Decline of the Matrism under the conquering influence of northern Patrists.

2000–60 BC (Age of Aries). Iron Age – circa 12th century BC. Age of the conquerors, Theban period in Egypt. Exodus of Hebrews. Eventual Hellenisation of Egypt. Rise of Rome.

60BC–Present. Advent of the Age of Pisces by astronomical calculation.

The Ammonite Foundation of Egypt furnished me with the following list, although they were careful to emphasize that they do not understand or observe western astrology. Their suggestion for each Age is therefore purely speculative, although this list assumes a new significance in the light of the above table (the question marks are theirs):

The Void of Ammun (Capricorn?)
The Aeon of Nut of Division (Aquarius?)
The Age of Life in the Sea (Pisces?)
The Age of Ra (Aries?)
The Manifested Ra (Taurus?)
The Reign of Us-Ar and Auset (Gemini?)

---

* Author's note: There would appear to be some confusion here between those whom the ancient records refer to as 'Shemsu-Hor' and, perhaps the fair-haired, blue-eyed Frisians, who possibly settled on both Egyptian and Greek shores during this period.

The Age of Retraction (Cancer?)
The Age of Nebt Sekhmet Montu and the destruction of Sea of
  Blood (Leo?)
The Age of Balance (Libra?)
The Age of Builders (Sagittarius?)

The absence of Virgo from this list fortifies the idea that an attempt
is being made to accommodate modern western astrology when
the Ammonite traditions obviously relate to a period of world
history which is much broader. The Scribe added the following
comment:

> The Book of Faith was not revealed or found by Heru-ta-ta-fu, Bringer
> of His Own Hope, until the Age of the Builders (pyramids?) . . .
> Tehuti was upon the earth from the time of the Age of Ra and Nebt
> Sekhmet Montu was upon the earth from the Age of the Manifested
> Ra. [5]

The Scribe then furnished me with a detailed story of the life (or
lives?) of the Goddess Sekhmet, who is seen as being the Neter
(god) who was entrusted by her father, Ra, with the task of
destroying the evils created by mankind. When I questioned the
Scribe concerning Atlantis he replied:

> We do not know the name 'Atlanteans' here. Perhaps they are 'The
> People of the Green Sea'? We know them to have become extinct
> shortly after Us-Ar's arrival on earth in the Sinai . . .

This would be towards the end of the Zodiacal Age of Scorpio,
when Mu is believed to have sunk and the Atlantean civilization
founded, although I rather suspect that we are dealing with two
different epochs here.

The Atlantic Ocean
And so we arrive at the final position for the Old Country: in the
region of the Atlantic Ocean itself, just as Plato described. Ignatius
Donnelly stated that in his lifetime (he died in 1901) there was
ample evidence from the seabed to suggest that Plato's island does
lie submerged in the Atlantic, and that the Azores were formerly
the peaks of its highest mountains. Donnelly wrote:

> Deep-sea soundings have been made by ships of different nations; the
> United States ship *Dolphin*, the German frigate *Gazelle*, and the

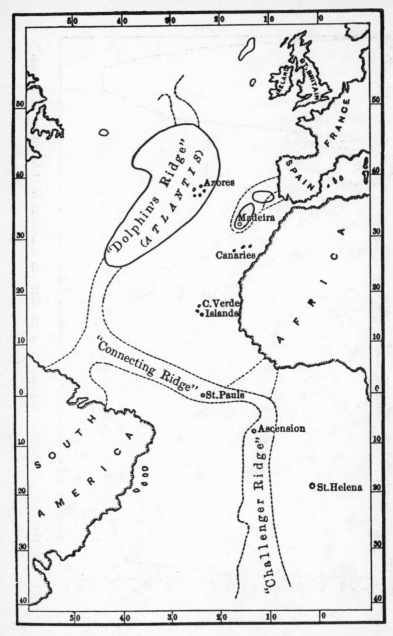

Figure 11a. Map of Atlantis, with its islands and connecting ridges, from deep-sea soundings.

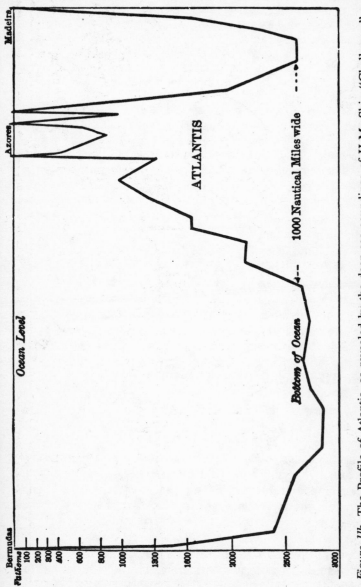

Figure IIb. The Profile of Atlantis, as revealed by the deep-sea soundings of H.M. Ship "Challenger" and the U.S. Ship "Dolphin".

British ships *Hydra*, *Porcupine*, and *Challenger* have mapped the bottom of the Atlantic, and the result is the revelation of a great elevation, reaching from a point on the coast of the British Islands southwardly to the coast of South America, at Cape Orange, thence south-eastwardly to the coast of Africa and thence southwardly to Tristan d'Acunha . . . It rises about 9,000 feet (2,743 metres) above the great Atlantic depths around it, and in the Azores, St. Paul's Rocks, Ascension, and Tristan d'Acunha it reaches the surface of the ocean.

Evidence that this elevation was once dry land is found in the fact that 'the inequalities, the mountains and valleys of its surface, could never have been produced in accordance with any laws for the deposition of sediment, nor by submarine elevation; but, on the contrary, must have been carved by agencies *acting above the water level*'.

(*Scientific American*, July 28th, 1977.)[6] (See figures 11a and 11b)

Geological Evidence

A transatlantic cable laid in 1898 suddenly snapped at a point under 47° N. and 29° W. of Paris, i.e. about 500 square miles north of the Azores. A cable-laying vessel searching for the broken cable between Brest and Cape Cod eventually retrieved it, but not without considerable difficulty. As a consequence, the location in question came to be known as Telegraph Plateau. During the course of this tedious operation some interesting facts emerged which go to support the idea that the Old Country was, indeed, where Plato said. High peaks and mountainous valleys were located on the sea floor 1,000 miles (1,609 kilometres) north of the Azores at a depth of 10,170 feet (3,100 metres), while dredging the ocean floor yielded fragments of vitreous lava, including a large piece of rock that was deposited in the Paris Museum. Strangely enough, it was some fifteen years before this specimen was finally examined by Paul Termier, director of the Oceanographic Institute at that time and recognized as a scientist of repute in his own country and in the world generally. Termier's conclusions?

1. That the specimen was of volcanic origin, and formed part of what must have been a considerable lava flow resulting from eruptions in the region of Telegraph Plateau.
2. That the specimen, which was of amorphous, vitreous and non-crystalline structure, must have solidified in free air, not in deep water.

3. That the whole region must have sank through more than 6,560 feet (2,000 metres) either at the same time as the volcanic eruption or very shortly afterward. The specimen was therefore evidence of a prehistoric catastrophe in the middle of the Atlantic.

4. Due to the mineralogical nature of the specimen, a tachylite, the fact that tachylites dissolve in sea water within about 15,000 years, and that the contours in said specimen appeared intact, the Atlantic catastrophe most likely occurred less than 15,000 years previously and probably considerably later than 13,000 BC. [7]

Of course, there were the usual disputations since scientists with set ideas are seldom happy if a fellow member of their profession dares to shake the portals of their hallowed establishment. The great scientist Hermann von Helmholtz (1821-94) was once heard to say: 'Neither the testimony of all the Fellows of the Royal Society, nor even the evidence of my own senses, would lead me to believe in the transmission of thought from one person to another independent of the recognized channels of sense . . . My mind is made up, and no evidence is going to change it.' The acceptance or rejection of empirical evidence, however, does not render it any the less valid, although in the final analysis like Helmholtz, we each tend to believe what suits us.

There have been many other strange tales connected with finds in the Atlantic. The crew of the British merchantman, *S.S. Jesmond*, for example, sighted huge numbers of dead fish and an unusual amount of surface mud in the sea some 200 miles west of Madeira and a similar distance south of the Azores. On the following day an uncharted island came into view, which had obviously risen suddenly from the depths of the ocean. The Captain, being consumed with curiosity, took a landing party ashore, which venture resulted in the discovery of a curious collection of artifacts, including:

> . . . bronze swords, rings, mallets, carvings of heads and figures of birds and animals, and two vases or jars with fragments of bone, and one cranium almost entire . . . [and] what appeared to be a mummy enclosed in a stone case . . . encrusted with volcanic deposit so as to be scarcely distinguishable from the rock itself. [8]

Since bronze is generally thought to have been invented around 3000 BC in the city states of Mesopotamia, there are two possible answers: First, that the Atlanteans possessed a knowledge of bronze centuries before the people of Europe or Mesopotamia, and secondly, that the artifacts were from a shipwreck. The stone sarcophagus, however, tends to discount the second possibility, while also inferring that the latter-day Atlanteans practised a system of sepulture similar to that later adopted by the ancient Egyptians. Donnelly quotes Sir John Lubbock (*Prehistoric Times*, p.59) as stating: 'The absence of implements made either of copper or tin seems to me to indicate that *the art of making bronze was introduced into, not invented in, Europe.*'[9]

In more recent times several erudite Russian writers and scholars have turned their attention to the subject of Atlantis, notably Professor Nicolai Zhirov, whose book *Atlantis* (1964) dealt with the historical and geological material available with special attention to its Atlantic location. A Soviet deep-sea expedition that took place early in 1974 was carried out by the *Academician Petrovsky*, a Soviet research ship engaged in photographing the sea floor in the region of the Horseshoe Archipelago. This U-shaped group of underwater mountains some 300 miles (483 kilometres) west of Gibraltar is in the same area as the strange island encountered by the crew of the *Jesmond*. The Soviet scientists took a considerable amount of photographs during this expedition which, when printed, showed massive stone walls, stone staircases, and other very obvious signs of a once thriving city. In fact, Professor Andrei Aksyonov, a leading scientist and deputy director of the Soviet Academy of Science's Institute of Oceanography, upon examining them later, commented: 'In my opinion these structures once stood on the surface.'[10] Needless to say, the Russians maintained their usual cloak of secrecy, *glasnost* not having appeared on the scene. More's the pity, however, as there is doubtless much information hidden away in some Soviet archives that has not been released. The late Egerton Sykes, an archaeologist and Atlantologist of distinction, maintained that the Russian secrecy was due to the fact that the pictures had been taken off the Azores, between Santa Maria and São Jorge, a strategically important location which was strictly out of bounds for them at the time, and that the *Petrovsky* was nothing more than a spy ship! Those interested in fuller details of the Russian finds are recommended to Berlitz' book, and to *Atlantis: Myth or Reality*.

Evidence collected from the ocean bed would appear to leave little doubt that part of the Atlantic Ridge was once above water, and that it provided a pleasant habitat for a people sufficiently civilized to erect large edifices and produce artifacts comparable to anything encountered in much later periods of history. Although scientists, scholars and Atlantologists have proffered several theories as to the cause of the Atlantean catastrophe, the various volcanic deposits encountered would also seem to suggest that seismic disturbances of cataclysmic proportions played a major role in its ultimate demise. Whether these were, as Dr Otto Muck has suggested, precipitated by impact with a foreign body – comet, planetesimal or asteroid – is open to debate, while believers in 'the wrath of the gods' must look to their myths for the relevant clues.

As to the exact location of the Old Country, David Wood in his book *Genisis*, using a combination of sacred geometry and mathematics, calculated the coordinates to be 42° 55' N. and 26° 6' W, but since he appeared to be concerned as much if not more with the metaphysical aspects of his study we may assume this reference to bear some relationship to the main source of Atlantean occult power, which was doubtless situated in the old capital. Besides, if we are to pay any heed to Plato's measurements the Atlantean continent was of a fair size, so consideration should, therefore, be given to a cross section of the Atlantic discoveries coordinates if we are to arrive at anything near an accurate assessment of its former position in the ocean that now bears its name.

The words of Heinrich Schliemann, the excavator of Troy, serve as an excellent conclusion to this chapter: 'I have come to the conclusion that Atlantis was not only a great territory between America and the West Coast of Africa, but the cradle of all our civilization as well!' [11]

Endnotes
1. Mooney, R. *Colony Earth*, p.133–4.
2. Hapgood, C. *Maps of the Ancient Sea Kings*, pp.174–7.
3. Ibid. p.178.
4. Mooney, R. *Colony Earth*, p.109.
5. Hope, M. *Ancient Egypt: The Sirius Connection*, p.219.
6. Donnelly, I. *Atlantis: The Antediluvian World*, p.46–9.
7. Muck, O. *The Secret of Atlantis*, p.144.
8. Berlitz C. *Atlantis*, p.78–9.
9. Op. cit. Donnelly, p.238.
10. Op. cit. Berlitz, C. p.86.
11. Michell, J. *The View Over Atlantis*, p.162.

5. ATLANTIS – THE ISLAND CONTINENT

Before considering the religion, sciences and general lifestyle of the peoples of Atlantis, it is necessary to establish the size of the island continent and the climatic conditions that rendered it such a paradise on earth. Aside from Plato's description of its proportions, and the evidence from the seabed which suggests that a large section of the mid-Atlantic ridge was once above ground, we have little to go on when it comes to the actual dimensions of the island continent. Also, there are still many people who, while professing to believe in its former existence, refer to it in terms of a 'lost city'. Working on the figures given by Plato, Atlantologists have estimated the Atlantean land mass to have occupied some 600,000 square miles (1,553,994 square kilometres) in area, which figure would appear to be compatible with the seabed contours. Plato describes Atlantis as 'larger than Asia and Libya together'. But it should be borne in mind that the Asia Plato knew is the Asia Minor of today, while Libya represented all of North Africa that was known to the ancients.

The German scientist Otto Muck judged the plain of Atlantis from northeast to southwest to have been some 370 miles (600 kilometres) and the average width 230 miles (370 kilometres). The superb climate he ascribed to the continent's encirclement by the Gulf Stream, which brought a never-failing supply of warm water while also helping to protect the land from the cold northerly winds. Muck, however, believed the mountainous region to be in the north, although his placing of the Royal City, near to the eastern coastline, agrees with Plato's description and my own recollection of its location. As I see it, the problem with many of the previous speculations regarding the climate and position of Atlantis is that they fail to take into account the different positions of the Poles and Equator. Edgar Cayce was one of the few psychics to observe this distinction. But then we have to consider the long period over which the Atlantean culture extended, and the many alterations that must have taken place as each successive generation added its own touch to the intensifying ethos.

Another problem that is frequently encountered when one is dealing with psychism and allied paranormal phenomena is the tendency to put the Atlantean tag on any memory of a former existence that the subject cannot place within the pages of established history. I have come across many gifted people with far memory, who have described 'Atlantis' to me in detail, only to find themselves corrected when confronted with pictures or descriptions of life in archaic Egypt, India, Turkey, Central America, Mu, or verdant Antarctica. There is now plenty of evidence to suggest that mankind has been around on this planet for far longer than many historians and archaeologists would have us believe, and I do not mean in our primitive form. Great civilizations have come and gone, some leaving not even a vestige of the knowledge they once possessed. Such giants of archaic civilization were often contemporaneous with pockets of extreme primitivism and savagery, in much the same way that the natives of Borneo, and the Indians of the Amazon rain forests still adhere to a Stone Age way of life on the doorsteps of the great metropolis of the so-called 'civilized' world.

A Different Hemisphere?

Cayce maintained that the Atlantean continent occupied a position between the Gulf of Mexico and the Mediterranean, although I am personally of the opinion that it also extended much farther north than most speculative maps suggest. His acknowledgement of the different position of the Earth's axis in those times may be evidenced in his statement:

> The extreme northern portions were then the southern portions, or the polar regions were then turned to where they occupied more of the tropical and semi-tropical regions; hence it would be hard to describe the change. The Nile entered into the Atlantic Ocean. What is now the Sahara was an inhabited land and very fertile. What is now the central portion of this country, or the Mississippi basin, was then

all in the ocean; only the plateau was existent, or the regions that are now portions of Nevada, Utah and Arizona formed the greater part of what we know as the United States. That along the Atlantic seaboard formed the outer portion then, or the lowlands of Atlantis. The Andean, or the Pacific Coast of South America, occupied then the extreme western point of Lemuria. The Urals and the northern regions of same were turned into a tropical land. The desert in the Mongolian land was then the fertile portion . . .

You see, with the changes when there came the uprising of the Atlantean land, and the sojourning southward with the turning of the axis, the white and yellow races came more into that portion of Egypt, India, Persia, and Arabia.[1]

(364–13; 1932)

Much of Cayce's work would appear to be unedited, which tends to make some of it difficult to pigeonhole from an empirical standpoint. I can, however, understand the reason for this, as successive generations of 'editors' might inadvertently alter the facts in their efforts to present a more pristine rendering of the English language. I rather gather that what he is referring to here is the position of Atlantis directly following the Mu-an (Lemurian) catastrophe, which would appear to concur with Warlow's hypothesis, and Hapgood's placing of the Poles during that era.

One of the problems with the Cayce readings would appear to be the subtle intrusion of his own religious upbringing and social conditioning, although any psychologist worth his or her salt would have no difficulty distinguishing this programming from the kind of information that would not normally have formed part of the educational vocabulary of a man of Cayce's background. His psychic gift is unquestionable, however, and a little logical application and empirical research soon serves to sort the wheat from the Biblical chaff.

The Atlantis I recall was positioned in what was then the southern hemisphere. Its northern parts were therefore very warm, its central plain enjoyed a Mediterranean-type climate but without the harsher winters to which such areas are sometimes exposed in this day and age, and its southernmost lands were mountainous and cooler, but with a temperate climate. Assuming that the Earth was slightly nearer to the sun, as has been previously suggested, the sea levels would have been lower, as Heezen has pointed out, and the direct sunlight obscured by a fine vapour-mist. One very clear picture of Atlantis, which I experienced in a hypnogogic state just prior to waking, was of a different kind of daylight from that of our present sunshine, the light being a silvery-white and devoid of the golden hue we tend to associate with fine, summer days. The air itself seemed to be rarer, finer and more moist, and the pull of gravity in less evidence.

The latter point raises the issue of height. The French scholar, Professor Denis Saurat, proposed that the proximity of the moon was connected with the phenomenon of height. Many myths and legends refer to the existence of people of great height in archaic times. Even the Bible states, 'There were giants on Earth in those days' (Genesis VI:4), which has been generally interpreted as meaning that at some period in the distant past people, on the whole, were much taller than they have been during the time of recorded history. The *Oera Linda Book* refers to the archaic Frisians as being seven feet (2 metres) tall and more, Professor Emery's skeleton (see Chapter 2) was also of these dimensions, and Greek mythology refers to the Titans as being of huge stature. Saurat tells us that fragments of colossal human or pre-human bones have been found in Java, Southern China and South Africa, and supplies the appropriate references. Exceptionally heavy stone implements (bifaces) weighing from 4 to 8 pounds (1.8 to 3.6 kilogrammes) have been discovered in Syria, Moravia and Morocco, suggesting that the users must have been at least 9 feet (2.7 metres) tall. [2]

So, assuming the Atlanteans to have averaged a height of 7 feet or more, what prompted this kind of growth, and why did it cease to apply in subsequent ages? The answer to this would appear to lie in the position of the Earth in those days, in relation to both the sun *and the moon*, assuming the moon was where we now see it! As regards the latter, however, there are areas of doubt which need to be explored if we are to obtain an accurate assessment of the kind of life enjoyed by the average Atlantean in the period between the sinking of Mu and the famous 'latter days' of the doomed Atlantic land mass.

Was Our Moon Always There?

Several scholars, including Saurat and H.S. Bellamy, have postulated that our planet did not always have a moon, but that our satellite was captured around the time of the sinking of Atlantis. Professor Hans Hoerbiger, whose theories were popular in the 1920s and 1930s, formulated a concept of a perpetual struggle between the forces of repulsion and attraction. This alternating tension between opposite principles, he postulated, also governs Earth and all living matter and determines human destiny. While some of his theories have since been disproved or discarded, chaos science has tended to confirm his general premise so, inasmuch as this may be applied to the Atlantean saga, he should be given a hearing. Hoerbiger suggested that prior to the arrival of our present satellite, Earth had another, smaller moon, which was eventually drawn into its orbit, the catastrophe created by its landing contributing to the sinking of Mu. It was the capturing of our present moon, however, which he envisaged as being originally a small planet in its own right, that was responsible for the Atlantean disaster.

Let us turn once again to myth and legend for the key to the lunar enigma. We have already noted that the disappearance of Atlantis was in some way connected with the matrist Age of Cancer, which is ruled by the moon. Was it then that lunar worship began? If so, where was the moon prior to that time, and is there any evidence of its existence? Colonel Braghine refers to the writings of certain ancient Classical authors, affirming that several millennia before their time a large and heavily populated continent existed in the region of the Indian Ocean between Africa, Arabia and Hindustan, and probably embracing many other lands (Gondwanaland and later Mu?). Since the moon was believed not to have existed in such times, the writers referred to the inhabitants of this legendary land as 'Preselenites'. Ancient tribal legends abound with tales of a time when there was no moon: Here are a few that were collected by Colonel Braghine:

- The legend of the Greeks concerning the Preselenites, who inhabited Gondwanaland before the appearance of the moon.
- The myth of the Chibchas of Columbia concerning Bohica, who created the moon after a great inundation in the Funza valley.
- The myth of the Bushmen, who affirm that a large continent west of Africa disappeared at an epoch when there existed *two* moons.
- The Mayan myth concerning a great calamity during which the Great Serpent, i.e. a certain celestial body, was ravished from the heavens.
- The myth of the Tupis, who affirm that the moon falls periodically upon the Earth and a new moon takes the place of the old one in the heavens.
- The Aravacs of Guiana affirm that the Great Spirit sent a

double calamity to the world: at first it was struck by fire and next a great flood covered the Earth.[3]

There would seem to be two celestial displacements mentioned here: the acquisition of a new satellite following the destruction of an earlier one, or the possible involvement of another extraterrestrial body such as a comet or asteroid. Hoerbiger might well have been basically correct in his double lunar theory; it was only in its justification that he erred. Since the destruction by fire would seem to belong to the Mu-an epic and the Flood to Atlantis, I am inclined to believe that the Phaeton episode described by Plato refers to the earlier cataclysm while the demise of the Atlantean continent was somehow connected with the moon. If Earth did not actually capture Lunar at that point then the two must have assumed a closer proximity, which would accord with Saurat's theory regarding the connection between gravity and the human height. Of course it could be argued that if the Earth was protected by a vapour mist during Atlantean times the sun would not have been seen as the golden orb we view today while the moon might not have been visible at all, especially if it were positioned differently in relation to the Earth. The problem with this theory is that the tribal and cultural sources which deny the existence of the moon did appear to be familiar with certain galactic and stellar formations, which rather suggests that they did have a fairly clear view of the night sky.

An interesting corollary to all this is that many of the ancient gods of Time were lunar – the Sumerian Sîn and the Egyptian deities Osiris and Khonsu, for example. The lunar Thoth (Tehuti) played a game of draughts with the moon which won him a seventy-second part of her light (1/72nd of 360 is exactly 5!) which he made into five extra days called 'epagomenal' from the Greek *epagomenos* (*epi* – upon, *agein* – to bring). It was during those five intercalary days that the five Great Neters of the old Egyptian religion – Isis, Osiris, Horus, Set and Nephthys – appeared on the scene. Are we being told that it was at the time of the acquisition of the epagomenal days, which occurred as a result of change in the orbit of our Earth in relation to the moon, that those great Bringers of Light, Ausar and Auset (Isis and Osiris) arrived on Egyptian soil? In other words, anticipating the eventual demise of their lands, members of the Atlantean priesthood or aristocracy fled their native country for the shores of Khemu (Egypt), which they knew was destined to survive the ensuing axis tilt.

The Epagomenal Days

The epagomenal Neters, it seems, were not all born on the same day, which suggests that their 'arrival' was over a period of time. Budge tells us that day one witnessed the birth of Osiris; day two saw the emergence of Horus; day three was Set's day; day four belonged to Isis, while day five was Nephthys' birthday. The first, third and fifth of the epagomenal days were considered unlucky, the second was neither lucky nor unlucky, while the fourth was said to be 'a beautiful festival of heaven and earth'.[4] The ancient Egyptians must, therefore, have experienced five different groups of Atlantean settlers, or colonizers as the case may be, during the time when Thoth was busily engaged in his famous board game. From this we may gather that the Atlantean catastrophe was foreseen several years prior to the final inundation, the impending celestial drama being fully visible to the Atlantean astronomers or astrophysicists. In other words, someone saw something coming when it was a long way off, and calculated mathematically when it was likely to strike the moon, causing that body to alter course and so disturb the orbital path of Earth. On the completion of Thoth's game, five extra days were added to the former calendar of 360, thus marking the moon as a significant point of calendar reference and, therefore, a God of Time.

How, then, did the moon acquire its feminine gender? Thereby hangs a tale, which, since it is not germane to our present subject matter, must remain untold. But for those readers who might care to know what happened, I would refer them to my book *Essential Woman: Her Mystery, Her Power*, which deals with the specific aspect of the feminine psyche as related to both solar and lunar energies and their cosmic variances.

Coming back to the 360-day year which I am proposing was operative during the Atlantean epoch, what evidence is there, if any, to support this theory?

- Several authorities have asserted that the circles of Avebury represent a calendar of 360 days, an extra five days being added later.
- The classic writings of the Hindu Aryans acknowledge a year of 360 days. The *Aryabhatiya*, an ancient Indian mathematical and astronomical work states: 'A year consists of 12 months. A month consists of 30 days.'[5]
- The ancient Babylonian year consisted of 12 months each of 30 days. Their zodiac was divided into 36 decans which

represented the position of the sun in relation to the fixed stars during a period of 10 days. The 36 decans therefore covered a 360-day year only. Ctesias observed that the walls of Babylon were 360 furlongs in circumference; 'as many as there are days in a year'.[6]

- According to the Ebers Papyrus, the old Egyptian year consisted of 12 months of 30 days each. The additional five days were added later.
- Plutarch wrote that in the time of Romulus (ancient Rome) the year was made up of twelve 30-day months.
- The old Mayan year consisted of 360 days, called a tun. Five days were later added, plus the customary day each fourth (leap) year. These extra days were called 'the days of nothing', which could be presumed to refer to a period of time during which the Earth stood still prior to tipping over into its present position. This also receives mention in the *Oera Linda Book*.
- The Incan year was divided into 12 quilla of 30 days. Again, we have the five days being added at the end with the extra one every fourth year. These extra days were considered by the Incans as unlucky or fateful.
- The ancient Chinese calendar consisted of 12 months each of 30 days. The extra days were brought in later and included in their geometry.

Scholars have often tried to explain away these inconsistencies, but their arguments seldom make sense since they are mostly based on the probability of errors in calculation. That so many cultures from different parts of the world should simultaneously commit the same errors, however, strains credulity somewhat, to say the least. The obvious answer is that the Earth's orbital position underwent a change at some point in the archaic past. Whether this was actually caused by a primary movement of the moon (the moon being struck by an extraterrestrial body of some kind), which in turn affected the position of Earth, or whether it was the other way round is, of course, open to speculation. Mooney tells us:

Since the moon is a smaller body than earth, and the distance between them much smaller than between the earth and the sun, the differences would have been even more noticeable in the case of the earth/moon system than in the case of the earth/sun system.

This would appear to have been the case. In several ancient sources it has been found that there were 4 9-day weeks to each lunar month, making a month of 36 days. The 9-day phase has been found in ancient Greek, Babylonian, Chinese, and Roman sources, among others. As these lunar computations did not fit with a year of 360 days, the calendars were altered to a 10-month year. This was an attempt to regulate the 'new' year to fit the 'old' 360 day year. [7]

Interestingly, the number 9 featured strongly throughout the whole of the Matrist, or Silver Age, the Celts in particular ascribing great magical power to it and associating it with the three aspects of their Triple Goddess – Maiden, Mother and Crone.

Different Sunrises

References to the sun rising and setting in positions that differ from the present east/west axis are to be found in many archaic writings. Ancient Chinese records mention a time when the sky suddenly began to fall northward and the sun, moon and planets changed their positions *after the Earth had been shaken*. Egyptian references bear witness to this, the tomb of Senmouth, architect to Queen Hatshepsut, displaying two star maps, one of which observes the present celestial placings while in the other they are completely reversed (see also Chapter 2, page 40). Other ancient records that refer to the Earth changing its position completely during some cosmic cataclysm include The Harris Papyrus, the Hermitage Papyrus of Leningrad, and the Ipuwer Papyrus. The zodiacal signs in the famous Zodiac of Denderah shows the sign of Leo at the vernal equinox (a position at present occupied by Aries), which could also be seen to contain a message.

From the *Oera Linda Book* we have the following description of what must surely be an axis tilt:

During the whole summer the sun had hid behind the clouds, as if unwilling to look upon the earth. There was perpetual calm, and the damp mist hung like a wet sail over the houses and the marshes. The air was heavy and oppressive, and in men's hearts was neither joy nor cheerfulness. In the midst of this stillness the earth began to tremble as if she was dying. The mountains opened to vomit forth fire and flames. Some sank into the bosom of the earth and in other places mountains rose out of the plain. Aldland, called by the seafaring people Atland, disappeared, and the wild waves rose so high over hill and dale that everything was buried in the sea. Many people were swallowed up by the earth, and others who had escaped the fire perished in the water. [8]

Assuming Atland to have occupied the position indicated by the ancient Frisian records, off the coast of Scandinavia in the area of the North Sea, it would seem logical to assume that their lands were destroyed at the same time that the last of the Atlantic continent went down. Since we now have evidence that lands in that area sank around 5000 BC, are we being given yet another hint as to the time of the Atlantean catastrophe which would seem to confirm Spence's premise of a double catastrophe separated by several centuries? (see map on page 30). Note that there is no mention of the approach of a celestial body with a fiery tale or any similar phenomena, although the *Oera Linda Book* does state that following this disaster the *climate changed overnight from subtropical to the colder temperatures experienced in present-day Scandinavia. Rivers altered their courses, whole forests were burned out, and many other countries were submerged. It was almost three years before these disturbances ceased completely, leaving the land with new contours and an entirely different climate.*

The Norse *Voluspa* offers more confirmation in the following verses:

Verse 3
Until the sons of Bur raised the ground
Created her, Midgarth, the myth.
The sun shone on stone battlements from the south,
The ground turned green and verdant with leek.

Verse 4
From the south the sun, the moon's companion,
Touched the edge of the heavens.
The sun did not know his halls.
The moon did not know her might.
The stars did not know their places. [9]

Here we have a clear allusion to the sun rising in the south, and to the subsequent displacement of both sun and moon, while the reference to the moon being unaware of her might suggests that this body exerted some powerful influence on the events taking place that was totally out of character with its previous role in relation to the celestial balance. The reference to the sun not knowing his halls and the stars being unaware of their places obviously alludes to their change in position *as seen from the earth*. As I see it, not only did the position of the Poles change, but *the Earth actually turned upside down* or rolled over!

Having offered some evidence to substantiate claims that Atlantis was a fair-sized island continent with a superb climate; that it was positioned in the Atlantic Ocean but, due to the different position of the axis of the earth in relation to the sun it lay in *what was then the southern hemisphere*, which meant that its warmest parts were in the north and its more cooler, mountainous lands in the south, how, then, was the land divided? Aside from Plato and the occasional snippet of information from the ancient classical writers, we have only inspiration, far memory and the collective unconscious to draw on. Here is a description given by Helio Arcanophus and channelled through Tony Neate, which I feel is as accurate as one is likely to get using this method of psychic communication. The period during which this High Priest reigned was during the Age of Virgo, when the country was under strict sacerdotal rulership, so it naturally differs considerable from Plato's Age of the Kings, which occurred considerably later:

The Atlantean continent was flat in the north and inclined to be dry although it was by no means barren. Most of the mountain ranges of the continent lay to the south and it is said that the topmost peaks coincide with the islands of the Azores; although it would be difficult to equate any existing land-masses with parts of the continent, as the topography changed so drastically at the time of the tilt. Its northern zone was extremely warm, its central or temperate zone enjoyed the type of climate you would associate with the South Sea Islands, and its southern zone was somewhat cooler – more like southern England or Northern France. These three zones were given names that resonated to their particular elemental atmospheres. The northern zone was called Portea, the central zone, Cintrala and the southern zone Usiqua. There were cities, towns and villages throughout the continent that were mainly circular in shape, well irrigated and beautifully kept. Colour was used profusely in both dwellings and temples, and sharp angles were always avoided.

The capital of the southern province was Kudra, while the northern province was dominated by Keriophis. Menocea was a large city in the northeast, while the nearest city to the capital itself was Mentis, to the east. The Atlantean civilization lasted for many thousands of years and many townships sprang up and crumbled during that time. A person who has a memory of Atlantis from an incarnation in the latter days would doubtless bring back many facets of experience that would contrast strongly with the experiences of those who were incarnate a century or so earlier; think of how architecture, clothing and life generally has changed over the past few hundred years in your present world.

The capital of Atlantis lay on the eastern side of the central zone, some twenty-five miles from the sea. This was built on the great river Chalid and was called Chalidocean.* It was sometimes known as 'the City of the Golden Gates' which name carried an esoteric rather than a secular meaning.

In the centre of Chalidocean were situated many great buildings such as art galleries, the houses of government and the great colleges where science and metaphysics were studied by the priests and their students. There were four waterways running through this great city, three of which were canalised from the river Chalid. Outside the city itself were great storage houses where grain and other commodities were stored on the advice of the priests. The Atlanteans did not build closely as you do today, for they knew the benefits that could be obtained from leaving large spaces of ground free. The grass, plants and trees that grew there purified the air and helped to keep the people strong and healthy. In the centre of this great city stood the great temple, complete with its blue-tiled courtyard, fountains and stately pillars. Therein glistened precious and semi-precious stones of every type, some of which you would not recognize today as they were peculiar to Atlantis as was the metal orichalcum. Orichalcum was like a pink version of gold and extremely beautiful. It was used much in external building because it did not tarnish and therefore needed little attention to preserve its pristine appearance. Jewels and precious metals did not have the same values for the Atlanteans of my day as they do for the peoples of today, for their country abounded in them and there was no monetary system such as you have to inflate their value. [10]

This channelling was given in the mid-1950s, long before I had effected a specialized study of Atlantis. I can also vouch for the fact that at the time Tony Neate had never read a book on the subject, or even heard of Plato's famous work with its descriptions of circular cities, canals and so forth. Nor had either of us ever heard of Edgar Cayce or his Foundation, so there must be some universal link with the collective unconscious that occasionally allows us access to these past scenarios. The more metaphysically-minded among us would probably refer to it as a dip into the Akashic Records, but since, at a given frequency, all Time is one,

---

*Diodorus Siculus refers to the capital city of Atlantis as Cercenes, which is pretty close to Helio Arcanophus' Chalidocean, given the numerous translations into different languages that it must have suffered over the ensuing centuries.

as mankind slowly masters the frequencies of Time's subtle energies, such prehistoric events will one day be open to viewing by all, by means thoroughly acceptable to the scientific community. After all, Atlantean magic and metaphysics were nothing more than advanced science, backed up by a technology, the knowledge of which is only just beginning to return to us via the agencies of quantum mechanics, cosmology and allied studies.

Endnotes
1. Cayce, E. *Edgar Cayce on Atlantis*, pp.53–4.
2. Saurat, D. *Atlantis and the Giants*, p.11.
3. Braghine, C. *The Shadow of Atlantis*, p.105.
4. Budge, E. A. Wallis. *The Gods of the Egyptians*, Vol. 2, p.109.
5. Mooney, R. *Colony Earth*, p.95.
6. Ibid. p.96.
7. Ibid. p.97.
8. Scrutton, R. *The Other Atlantis*, p.48.
9. Muck, O. *The Secret of Atlantis*, p.176.
10. Dee, N. and Taylor, S. *Atlantis, Past and to Come*, pp.22–4.
11. Spence, L. *The Occult Sciences in Atlantis*, p.87.

6. THE PEOPLES OF ATLANTIS

Although the information given in this chapter may appear at first glance to be either purely speculative, or based on something as empirically insubstantial as a series of psychic impressions, this is not entirely the case. We have already established that skeletons averaging seven feet tall have been discovered in Egypt, but that is not all. The results of the search for genetic identification among short sequences of DNA that have survived 7,000 years in bodies preserved in a marshy bog in what is now Little Salt Spring, Florida have baffled scientists. By examining the DNA in minute detail and comparing it with that of present-day human races, the bog people's genealogy could be partly traced. One piece of the ancient DNA matches that found in more than half of today's American Indians living in the southwestern United States, and most modern Asians. This marks out the bog people as the Asian-Indian stock from which all Amerindians are believed to have descended. However, also present is a portion of DNA, extremely rare in modern worldwide populations, indicating that they had an ancestry unknown in the New World. The scientists hope that further research will throw light on both the origin of the enigmatic genetic 'stranger' and on how these people migrated to their marshy corner of America from some distant home in Asia. The Asian DNA could be seen as being of Mu-an or Gondwanian origin, and the unidentified strain Atlantean, although the scientific establishment will no doubt come up with its own explanation in due course.

Blood tests on five Inca mummies in the British Museum showed that three of them possessed traces of Blood Group A, which is utterly foreign to the South American Indian, while none of them displayed the rhesus-negative factor dominant in the Basques and Berbers. From this we may deduce that the Inca kings either did not belong to the aboriginal population of South America, or resulted from a cross-breeding with the Atlantean missionaries/culture bringers who had landed on those shores.

An Extraterrestrial Gene?

A third explanation which will, no doubt, appeal to those who favour an extraterrestrial interpretation of the 'missing link', would be that the unidentified gene derived from those mysterious 'sons of god' who, either by premeditation or chance, deposited it among *Homo sapiens* during their matings with 'the daughters of men'. While I am prepared to concede that some of us may well carry an E.T. gene, the idea that little green men, or tall, fair, handsome specimens come to that, popped out of a UFO and obliged the local maidens, does tend to strain credulity somewhat. What is probably more likely is that the strain was introduced either via panspermia as Hoyle suggests, or by the process of spiritual genetic refinement – the introduction into the species of higher evolved psyches who effected the designated somatic mutation. Doubtless, this process would have been accompanied by an evolutionary quantum leap which affected the whole planet. It would be logical, therefore, to assume that one such mutation occurred at the time of the formation of the Atlantean state following the sinking of Mu and the subsequent break-up and reformation of the earth's landmasses worldwide. Another mutation could well have occurred prior to the rise of Mu. I am inclined to believe that such evolutionary movements are externally orchestrated. In other words, since the cosmos functions as an intelligent whole, and not in isolated pockets as many people have tended to believe, extraterrestrial events must also have an effect on evolutionary patterns on this planet, just as the emanations or energies emitted from Gaia, and all that dwell upon her, in turn affect the rest of the solar system and galaxy.

The Atlantean Genetic Pool

Creation myths are a subject unto themselves, and I am only referencing them if they relate specifically to the Atlantean or Mu-an/Lemurian episodes. One such myth that does fall into this category is, however, that of the Frisians, in that it may help to give us an idea of what the original inhabitants of the island continent looked like, while also confirming some of the findings of modern science. According to the *Oera Linda Book*, the first beings, created from the joint energies of Mother Earth and the god Wr'Alda, were three daughters: Lyda, Finda and Frya, in that order. This Wr'Alda is referred to in the ancient Frisian texts in a monotheistic vein, and yet Alda is surely a derivative of Aldland, the original name of Atland. It is possible that Aldland, in turn, derived from 'Old Land', or an equivalent sounding name, and referred to Atlantis. This would mean that the ensuing Creation myth would, like many others, cover a history of world evolution as seen through the eyes of a particular race of people – the Atlanteans!

But to return to our three Earth Mothers: Lyda is described as black, with hair that curled like a lamb's; Lyda was yellow, and her hair was 'like the mane of a horse', and Frya was white, and '. . . the blue of her eyes vied with the rainbow . . . Like the rays of the sun shone the locks of her hair'.[1]

The suggestion here is that the first hominids were black, a fact that could be seen as confirmed in genetic evidence produced by Professor Allan Wilson, a biochemist at the University of California at Berkeley, that all present-day humans are related to an African woman who lived 200,000 years ago. The second wave, described as yellow, appears to relate specifically to the Slavic and Mongolian peoples, and the third to the fair-haired Nordic type, often called 'Aryan'. The Aryan peoples are believed to have invaded India and parts of Europe thousands of years ago, bringing with them their tales of wars in the heavens, struggles between different deities and strange conflagrations into which nuclear connotations are often read, all of which are narrated in the *Mahabharata*. Mooney quotes the *Zend-Avesta*, Holy Book of the Persians, as stating that Ormuzd, the Good Deity, '. . . gave the Aryans 16 countries, described as a region of delight, as their home. Ahriman, the Evil One, turned their home into a land of death and cold, partly by means of a great flood.'[2]

However, the Aryan legend could apply to either Atlantis or Mu, as Churchward opined that the original Mu-ans were a white race, which eventually interbred with peoples of darker complexion. There is a school of thought that proposes the white people originally to have come from what we now see as the Arctic and Antarctic regions, which were once well-populated, verdant lands.

Following the Atlantean axis tilt they moved south into Scandinavia, northern Europe and northern Asia (or northwards from the Antarctic regions as the case may be), while the specific branch of their people that had settled on the Atlantean land mass prior to the Mu-an catastrophe was mostly destroyed at the time of the Flood. I say 'mostly' because, for reasons we shall examine shortly, the Atlanteans were careful to ensure that their genes were preserved, and it was for this reason, and not for economic gain, mastery, or any other such material considerations that the priestly rulers *originally* embarked upon their programme of colonization.

Hapgood cites the work of Dr William F. Warren, President of Boston University, whose sensational book *The Cradle of the Human Race at the North Pole* was published in 1898 by Houghton, Mifflin & Co. of Boston. Hapgood assures us that Dr Warren's work was not a piece of sensationalism or pseudo-science, but '. . . a very serious systematic work for which he drew upon a very rich knowledge of ancient languages and literatures as well as on scientific studies in geography, geology, climatology, palaeontology and anthropology. He cites evidence from Japanese and Chinese literature, and from Iranian, Akkadian, Assyrian, Babylonian, Egyptian and Greek thought.'[3] The work served as an inspiration for the Vedic scholar, B.G. Tilak, whose book *The Arctic Home of the Vedas* was first published in 1903 and subsequently in 1925 and 1956 in Poona, India. Tilak proposed that the Vedas were obliged to abandon their polar home because of the coming of the Ice Age.

Since there is little land in the area of the North Pole, Hapgood has suggested that the Vedas actually came from Antarctica, the journey from that land to the southernmost tip of India being highly feasible. However, for all we know at some point in the distant past there may well have been considerably more land above water in those regions. After all, if we are to believe that land masses the size of Mu and Atlantis can disappear during an axis tilt, why not the original Vedic lands in what is now the North?

Hapgood assumes the Ice Age referred to by Tilak to have been the last Ice Age in North America, called the 'Wisconsin Glaciation' and explains:

In my book, *The Path of the Pole*, I have shown by radiocarbon and other evidence that this ice age began at least 50,000 years ago, and this, of course, would imply an enormous age for the Vedic literary tradition.[4]

The present ice sheet, on the other hand, has been dated by Hapgood at between 10,000 and 15,000 years ago, ancient maps having shown that Antarctica was free of ice and totally navigable prior to then.

The Vedic culture, like that of Atlantis, obviously originated from an even earlier society but, due to the considerable topographical changes to our planet, archaeological or allied research in lands that are now ice-locked, is hardly rewarding. Perhaps we will have to wait until the next tilt when the Poles change their positions yet again (which, according to the psychic pundits, is not all that far off) before the mystery can be eventually solved.

Not all researchers are of the opinion that the Atlantean race was white, however, and in the latter days it would appear to have been decidedly mixed. Colonel Braghine believed European culture to be inherited from some western race of the dolichocephalic (long-headed) type who arrived in the Mediterranean basin from somewhere beyond Gibraltar during the Neolithic period. He noted that all mysterious nations of the Mediterranean basin, apart from the Semitic peoples (Arabs and Jews), were remarkable for the reddish colour of their skin and scantiness of beard. Such people were pre-Egyptians, Pelasgi, Lycians, Crete-Aegeans, Phoenicians, Philistines, Kaftorim and Masinti on this side of the Atlantic, and Toltecs and Mayas on the other. He added that the Cro-Magnon people are also believed to have been reddish-brown. The Aryans, on the other hand, were brachycephalic (shorter and more round-headed). [5]

However, stories of 'white men who came from the gods' are more frequent than those of red men, although I rather suspect this was because most of the Atlantean missionaries were priests or scientists, the caste system being strictly observed among certain elements of the priesthood right up to the latter days. Although this might appear as sociological bias according present-day thinking, their reasons were vastly different, as the state of the world in those days bears no comparison with the conditions prevalent in modern society. Braghine lists the following legendary white visitors who were great reformers, leaders and missionaries, preaching a doctrine of pacifism, non-violence, brotherly love and law and order:

In Peru: Manco Capac, Viracocha and Pachacamac;
In Columbia: Bochica.

Among the Tupis: Tupan.

In Yucatan: It-Zamna, or Zamna;

In Mexico: Quetzal-Coatl (called in Guatemala, 'Gucumatz', and in Yucatan 'Cuculcan'):

In Brazil and Paraguay: Zume (called by the Caribs 'Tamu', by the Arovacs 'Camu' and by the Carayas 'Caboy'). [6]

The Peruvian myth concerning Viracocha resembles the Columbian myth concerning Bochica.

All these teachers were sages who hailed from an unknown land *in the east*. They were all fair-skinned and blue eyed, some of them were bearded, and they were clothed in white or pale blue garments – the colours of the Atlantean priesthood as distinguished from that of Mu, which favoured the stronger tones of red.

I find myself disagreeing with Churchward as regards the colour of the ancient Mu-an people. These, I feel, were the original red people. The name 'Adam' is said to mean 'red', and since Mu preceded Atlantis, this could have given rise to later myths regarding a race of Adamic or 'red' people. In fact, sorting the two myths and their relevant prehistoric cultures from one another is no easy task. Churchward, Donnelly, and other scholars of distinction and erudition have fallen into the trap of confusing the two, so much careful observation is needed when dealing with this issue.

The ancient Egyptians, who are believed by some authorities to have been red themselves, recognized four main races of men – the red, yellow, black and white. Donnelly tells us:

> They themselves belonged to the 'Rot', or red men; the yellow men they called 'Namu' – it included the Asiatic races; the black men were called 'Nahsu', and the white men 'Tamhu'. [7]

Ancient Aryan writings also refer to the same four races, the four castes of India being founded on these distinctions in colour. The Sanskrit word for colour, *varna*, actually means caste.

An Atlantean Blood Group?

I have often heard it said (and seen it written) that the rhesus-negative factor is in some way connected with Atlantis. The Mayans, Ossets of the Caucasus, certain Berber tribes and, of course, the Basques, carry this distinction, although not within the same blood groups. The Basques have a high frequency of the O group, the A group being extremely rare among them. Some authorities believe the combination of O blood group with the Rhesus-negative factor relates to an almost pure survival of Cro-Magnon man, skeletal remains showing evidence of facial similarities. Another school of thought sees the Cro-Magnons as a European import from Atlantis, but I am inclined to disagree with this, and have made my case in greater detail in *Atlantis: Myth or Reality?* Braghine noted that the Basque language, which is dissimilar from any other European tongue, strongly resembles Japanese. This is hardly surprising, since the Japanese are believed to be descended from Mongolian stock which, in turn, was of Tungus origin, and the Tungus are known to have migrated eastward.

Of all the known blood groups, O is the most common, and those populations with a high frequency of O are to be found in northeastern Europe (Wales, Scotland, Ireland, Iceland), southwest Africa, parts of Australia and, most notably, Central and South America. North American Indians also have a high frequency of O, with its accompanying *O* gene, although the *A* gene is sometimes found amongst them. The B blood group is mostly to be found in eastern Europe, among the Mongolian and Oriental races, as well as in the peoples of central Asia and the Indian subcontinent. Donnelly makes an interesting observation that would appear to be relevant to this blood group:

> If a congregation of twelve representatives from Malacca, China, Japan, Mongolia, Sandwich Islands, Chili, [sic] Peru, Brazil, Chickasaws, Comanches, etc., were dressed alike, or undressed and unshaven, the most skillful anatomist could not, from their appearance, separate them.
> (Fontaine, *How the World Was Peopled*, pp.147 and 244)[8]

Frequencies of the A blood group and consequently the *A* gene are particularly high in Scandinavia and parts of central Europe. Regarding the *A* gene, geneticist A. E. Mourant has this to say:

> . . . if we consider only the broad distribution of *A* in the world as a whole and disregard minor details, it becomes obvious that a higher frequency of *A* is something especially European. The high *A* people may have come into Europe from the east in late prehistoric times, but if so, they do not appear to have left any extensive roots behind, for nowhere in Asia, except Anatolia and Armenia, do we find any

large populations with *A* frequencies as high as in parts of Europe. In North Africa, which lies on another route for early man into western Europe, frequencies of *A* are notably low. [9]

This statement, from one of the leading geneticists of our day, surely implies that the A blood group is *not* of Mu-an or Lemurian origin, neither would it appear to carry Cro-Magnon associations. (Was it not Armenia where the Ark was supposed to have landed following the Flood – Atlanteans fleeing from their sinking land?). Both the Incan and Egyptian royal families appeared to carry the A group as distinct from the O group mostly found among their countrymen, and myth and legend supply us with several pieces of evidence to the effect that the Atlantean aristocracy were careful as to whom they allowed into their genetic pool, especially during the earlier days of Atlantean history. The Aztecs, like the Toltecs and Nahautlacas, tell of their ancestors having come from a land called Aztlan or Atlan. According to the *Popul Vu* (the sacred book of the Quiche of Guatemala, sometimes referred to as the Bible of the Mayas), after their migration from Aztlan the three sons of the King of the Quiches, upon the death of their father, '. . . determined to go as their fathers had ordered to the East, on the shores of the sea whence their fathers had come, to receive the royalty, "bidding adieu to their brothers and friends and promising to return."' [10] This would, of course, account for the presence of the A blood group in the Inca mummies.

The old Frisian tale of the three founders of the black, yellow and white races respectively does seem to fit in with the three main blood groups, Lyda's people being predominantly O, Finda's people B, and Frya's race A. And so the Frisian annals, in keeping with other ancient literature classified as 'mythological', would appear to hint at a scientific knowledge only comparable to that of the present day or, perhaps, even more advanced! There are also other, lesser known and much rarer blood groups, but since their ratio in relation to world population is extremely low, a consideration of the areas of population concerned would add little to our present subject matter. Also, since most of these genetic studies have been effected, the availability of worldwide travel to so many people in recent times has resulted in the intermingling of the various blood groups to the extent that their lands of origin become difficult to establish. The aforementioned can therefore be taken only as guidelines as far as our Atlantean inquiry is concerned, although I am sure that a geneticist with the right qualifications and experience could probably effect a better judgement in the matter.

In summary, it would seem that during the Ages of Libra and Virgo, the Atlantean stock consisted mainly of red- or yellow-skinned, brown- or green-eyed Mu-an types, and the fair, freckled or golden-skinned, violet or blue eyed people, who were the ruling class not because of the colour of their skin, but because they happened to be the tribe that civilized and brought culture to their inhospitable piece of land prior to the Mu-an inundation. Donnelly asserts that there were originally two distinct white races, one of which was primarily fair- or blonde-haired and the other red- or auburn-haired. Both appear to have been present in Atlantis from the earliest times and to have interbred over the long years of Atlantean history.

In later times, if we are to believe Plato and other writers, there was an influx of people from the black and yellow races, all of whom apparently dwelt together in harmony, and without the racial tensions we experience today. Interestingly, the fair Atlanteans that I 'recall' were of a slightly Mongolian appearance, having high cheekbones and slanted eyes, this feature appearing in both the blonde and red-haired strains. The red or Mu-an people, however, did not appear to exhibit this particular feature, their eyes being somewhat straighter and their foreheads more backward sloping.

The Atlanteans were a very tall people, averaging seven feet or more and, with their regime of a balanced diet, plenty of exercise, fresh air and sun, they did not tend towards corpulence. During the Age of Leo, when Atlantis opened up its shores to world trade, other O blood group peoples such as the Berbers and Basques to the east, and certain Indian tribes to the west, intermarried with native Atlanteans, thus implanting the *A* gene into certain of the O blood groupings. Therefore anyone who, for example, finds him or herself to be of the A blood group but carrying the rhesus-negative factor, could claim Cro-Magnon/Atlantean ancestry, as in the case of the Egyptian Ammonites. Equally, a person of O blood group carrying Atlantean genetic markers might feel an affinity for the Old Country, although they would only sustain a far memory if the particular gene they had inherited carried the racial memory-imprint.

There is a great deal more that could be said on the subject of blood groups, but much of it is too technical for a work of this nature, and those interested in discovering their genetic past are recommended to Mourant's mammoth tome (see Bibliography). I must warn you, though, that there is a long waiting list, since it is the definitive medical work on the subject.

A System of Writing?

Did the Atlanteans possess a system of writing and, if so, what happened to it? I think there is little doubt that the peoples of the Old Country enjoyed a comprehensive system of communication, both written and oral. Donnelly cites the following pieces of information concerning pre-Flood writing:

> The Hebrew communicators on Genesis say, 'Our rabbins assert that Adam, our father of blessed memory, composed a book of precepts, which were delivered to him by God in Paradise.' (Smith's *Sacred Annals*, p.49). That is to say, the Hebrews preserved a tradition that the Ad-ami, the people of Ad or Adlantis, possessed, while yet dwelling in Paradise, the art of writing. It has been suggested that without the use of letters it would have been impossible to preserve the many details as to dates, ages and measurements, as of the ark, handed down to us in Genesis. Josephus, quoting Jewish tradition, says, 'The births and deaths of illustrious men, between Adam and Noah, were noted down at the time with great accuracy.' (Ant., *lib.* 1, *cap.* iii, s. 3.) Suidas, a Greek lexicographer of the eleventh century, expresses tradition when he says, 'Adam was the author of arts and letters.' The Egyptians said that their god Anubis was an antediluvian, and 'wrote annals *before* the Flood.' The Chinese have traditions that the earliest race of their nation, prior to history, 'taught all the arts of life and wrote books.' 'The Goths always had the use of letters' and Le Grand affirms that before or soon after the Flood 'there were found the acts of great men engraved in letters on large stones.' (Fosbrooke's *Encyclopaedia of Antiquity*, vol. 1, p.355.) Pliny says, 'Letters were always in use.' Strabo says, 'The inhabitants of Spain possessed records written before the Deluge.' (Jackson's *Chronicles of Antiquity*, vol. iii, p.85). Mitford's *History of Greece* (vol. 1, p.121) says, 'Nothing appears to us so probable as that it (the alphabet) was derived from the antediluvian world.'[11]

The reference to Paradise is an interesting one for, although commonly associated with the popular religious idea of a state of bliss in some celestial dimension, the word actually derives from 'Avestan *pairi-daezaē*, circumvallation, walled-in park: (*pairi* around + *daezaē* wall)'.[12] In other words, some kind of circular enclosure (note Plato's description of the Atlantean capital).

Richard Heinberg's book *Memories and Visions of Paradise*

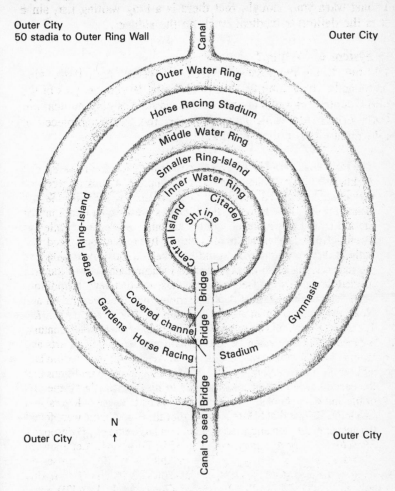

Figure 12. The shape and structure of the capital city of Atlantis, according to Plato's description.

provides some interesting insights into the Paradise theme, especially at the psychological and metaphysical levels, while also emphasizing the power of the collective unconscious and the memories contained therein that relate specifically to the early history of our species.

There are other references, notably in the G.R.S. Mead translations of the body of literature entitled *Thrice Greatest*

Hermes, which abounds with references to pre-Flood books. Clement of Alexandria, for example, wrote that the gods Hermes (Thoth), Ptah, and Imhotep once lived amongst men in Egypt to which they came from a land before the Flood. Hermes, the learned father informs us, brought from his homeland certain books of a medical and priestly nature that were absolutely indispensable. These were forty-two in number, thirty-six of which contained the whole wisdom discipline of the ancient priesthood while the remaining six were medical treatises which covered specialized aspects of healing, these being: 37 – The Constitution of the Body; 38 – Diseases; 39 – Instruments; 40 – Drugs; 41 – Eyes; and 42 – The Maladies of Women. [13] Mead also tells us:

> It is proposed then to make a few extracts concerning the Egyptian dynasties from the Books of Manetho. [This Manetho] being high priest of the heathen temples in Egypt, based his replies [to King Ptolemy] on the monuments which lay in the Seriadic country. [These monuments] he tells us, were engraved in the sacred language and in the characters of the sacred writing by Thoth, the first Hermes; after the Flood they were translated from the sacred language into the then common tongue, but [still written] in hieroglyphic characters, and stored away in books by the Good Daimon's son and the second Hermes, father of Tat – in the inner chambers of the temples of Egypt. [14]

The Greek use of the word 'daimon' does not carry the same connotations as the later Christian meaning, being employed in Classical times to describe the spirits of demi-gods, devas and, latterly, the souls of the great heroes of the Hellenistic past. The reference to two languages is also deserving of consideration. The 'sacred language', for example, could either have been some tongue exclusive to the priesthood or sacerdotal liturgy (similar to the Church Latin that was employed in Roman Catholicism until comparatively recently), or it could have been the old Atlantean tongue which in the time of the second Hermes was no longer spoken (see also Chapter 9, page 145).

Mead's scholarly work abounds with similar quotes from fragments of ancient scripts that he laboriously pieced together: the works of the early classical writers and historians; and the dissertations of the Church Doctors and Fathers who saw fit to disagree with the earlier schools of belief but, in so doing, familiarized their readers with the details. I have dealt with

Manetho's 'Sothis' in my book *Ancient Egypt: The Sirius Connection*, since the Seriadic land referred to is, of course, Egypt.

Speculation as to the nature of the old Atlantean tongue has produced a variety of ideas and suggestions, some of which have been based on a philological study of linguistics. From the evidence assembled (see *Atlantis: Myth or Reality?* for tables, comments and sources) it would seem that at some point in the dim and distant past there did appear to be some conformity of tongue. Separate forms of expression subsequently developed when groups of people became isolated during the various upheavals that occurred in the early days of man's existence on Earth. This is often read as evidence for the obviously metaphorical legend of the Tower of Babel, but then there is usually an element of truth in most mythology, and ancient Hebrew legends are no different from those of Greek, Egyptian, or Sumerian origin in that each contributes some small piece to the whole prehistoric jigsaw. I am sure that once we come to terms with the true nature and energy of Time we will obtain a much clearer picture of what the ancients were recording for posterity, doubtless never dreaming of how their words, taken too literally, would be used as instruments of torture, persecution and self-righteousness!

Endnotes

  1. Scrutton, R. *The Other Atlantis*, p.29.
  2. Mooney, R. *Colony Earth*, p.137.
  3. Hapgood, C. *Maps of the Ancient Sea Kings*, p.229.
  4. Ibid. p.229.
  5. Braghine, A. *The Shadow of Atlantis*, p.148.
  6. Ibid. pp.31–2.
  7. Donnelly, I. *Atlantis: The Antediluvian World*, p.194.
  8. Ibid. p.196.
  9. Mourant, A.E. *Distribution of Human Blood Groups*, 2nd Edition, p.62.
  10. Op. cit. Donnelly, p.106.
  11. Op. cit. Donnelly, p.236.
  12. *Reader's Digest Great Illustrated Dictionary*, Vol. 2, p.1235.
  13. Mead, G.R.S. *Thrice Greatest Hermes*, Vol. 3, p.225.
  14. Mead, G.R.S. *Thrice Greatest Hermes*, Vol. 1, p.104.

7. SCIENCE IN ATLANTIS

Some readers might see this as the point in my narrative at which logic flies the coop and the fairy tales begin. This will, of course, depend on whether or not you believe in the Atlantean legend but, should you fall into the sceptical category, then why not treat the following as a fascinating story from which modern society could possibly learn much.

The first thing one has to remember when thinking in terms of Atlantean science is that in those times there was no distinction between physics and metaphysics, astrology and astronomy, and the various schools of healing. All came under the jurisdiction of the Atlantean priesthood, and the novitiate was often required to sharpen his or her wits on both right- and left-brain hemisphere studies. There is a mistaken idea among some psychics that the ancient Atlanteans were predominantly right brain-orientated, which is utter nonsense. Their command of geometry, chemistry, mathematics, crystallography, geology, physics, cosmology, astronomy and architecture belies this as we shall see. On the other hand, they were sufficiently intuitive to comprehend the nature of Gaia, for whom they had their own name (see Chapter 8), and to observe the life force in natural phenomena and all things from the quantum worlds to the infinity of the cosmos. Several of our leading scientists today who sustain metaphysical leanings incline towards the belief that the sharp division between the rational and the intuitive is responsible for many of the problems facing us in modern society. Were we more spiritually aware and humanely motivated we might not have proceeded about the systematic torture and rape of the body of Gaia that has been effected by the demands of modern-day materialism. But then the pendulum 'twixt Order and Chaos is destined to make one of its inevitable swings from one extreme to the other, for such is the nature of the Universe, which also proceeds along the matter/anti-matter sine wave, or 'Big Bang/Big Crunch' theory, as some prefer to say. As the Atlantean priesthood was also aware, it is these alternations that provide the testing ground for our evolutionary progress via the soma, awakening us to cosmic awareness and eventually spiritual individuation (union with the anti-particle), thus alleviating the need for further 'particle' (material) experience (see my *Time – The Ultimate Energy*).

There were three grades of scientist-priests: discoverers, researchers and technologists. The first of these were the 'ideas' people, who could possibly be equated to the 'think-tank' professors of today; the second group were those who set about implementing the ideas via various avenues of research; and the technologists effected the final outcome. I have used modern terminology here as there are no words in present-day language that are anywhere near to the Atlantean originals, and it is necessary to give at least a broad idea of the kind of disciplines involved.

So, assuming the ancient Atlantean priesthood to have had a fair knowledge of science comparable to, and in some areas, ahead of what we have today, what did they know and from where did they obtain their information? What needs to be made quite clear at this point is that magic as an isolated study *did not exist in Atlantis*. All came under the heading of natural *science* and, as such, functioned according to cosmic laws. Many of these laws, especially those related to what we view as the insubstantial or metaphysical worlds, were understood. There was, therefore, no such thing as superstition, as there was a logical answer to all things. Early Atlantean logic was not tainted by dogma, however. In other words, unlike many people of today, the peoples of those times had not been programmed into set religious moulds from which they feared to escape into the insecurity of the 'unknown'. To the average Atlantean the universe was there to be acknowledged and explored, and if he or she felt inspired to pursue that exploration via the path of knowledge *accompanied by wisdom*, then the State Priesthood was open to anyone with the necessary talent and mental application, all education being completely free. What, then, were the qualifications required for entry into this exclusive ruling body, and who decided the suitability or otherwise of the applicants?

The Rite of Judgement

I have often heard it said that in a sacerdotally-ruled society the general populace is subjected to the dictatorship of the priesthood, who would then employ 'superstitious means' to designate every person's place in society, which procedure ensured that no one stepped out of line and rattled the sabres of revolution. This was not the case in Atlantis, however, since the so-called 'superstitious means' were anything but that. What actually happened was this: the Atlanteans were fully aware of the nature of what we now call quantum mechanics, while also possessing an advanced knowledge of sonics and genetics. By understanding that certain laws of physics operated exactly the same way in the human experience as they do in every other avenue of existence, the scientist-priests were able to measure the precise sonic, genetic, particle and wave frequencies of each individual. This information was then incorporated into a kind of composite 'energized graph' (the equivalent of the modern-day computer?). The graph was then matched against similar graphs that had been erected for a variety of callings from the most intellectually demanding to the most menial. This allowed each individual to be comfortably slotted into the area for which his or her talents were best suited or, as the more metaphysically-minded among us might say, their correct karmic path. In case you start visualizing Atlantean priests busy at their keyboards feeding the relevant information into some giant terminal, let me hasten to assure you that this was not the case at all. The probe was effected by a priest of the Order of The Divine Ancestor Ta-Khu, who was designated Master of Time, and could be equated with the Egyptian Tehuti (Thoth), Lord of The Divine Library of Akasha. The Judgement took place at the age of three, when all parents were obliged to present their children at the temple for the assessment to be made.

The Atlantean scientist-priests were also familiar with the true nature and energy of Time, but this knowledge was reserved for the very few since it carried a potential for personal danger. Anyone entering the circuits of Time without an intimate knowledge of their functioning was liable to become lost in a timeslip or timewarp. This fate was believed by the priesthood to be as terrible as anything we can imagine today, since it could encapsulate its victims in a limbo of spiritual isolation and suffering that could involve centuries in earth time. This was one of many reasons why the Atlanteans' most advanced scientific knowledge was kept completely secret – or was it? The answer to that must be yes *and* no, since some of it was incorporated into a series of subliminal symbols, the deeper meaning of which could only be understood and interpreted by someone at a certain level of spiritual or cosmic maturity. And yet these symbols were available to everyone; there was nothing secret about them, and some of them have survived to this very day via those mystery schools that had their origins among the Atlantean colonists. Over the centuries many of these sacred scientific glyphs have been relegated to the category of superstitious nonsense, whereas they are, in fact, time-capsules, due to be opened, explored and understood at given points in the history and evolution of our planet. I shall be dealing with some of these in a subsequent chapter although I must make it quite clear that, while I am cognizant with the fact that they were designed to function at multiple levels, and it will be this aspect of their energies that I shall be explaining, I make no claim to holding all the answers.

Science in Everyday Life

The Atlanteans incorporated their scientific knowledge into the everyday life of their peoples so that all could share from the benefit of their scholarship. By this means all power supplies were free; no monetary system was required; and medical facilities were free and open to all including animals, plants and trees – certain branches of the priesthood specialized in different areas just as we have orthopaedic specialists, veterinary surgeons and botanists today. Sacred geometry featured strongly in the dwellings of all from the highest ruler to the lowliest worker in the fields. There were no factories as such and, therefore, no mass production, but all crafts and similar skills were fully acknowledged and seen as essential to the whole. No job of work was seen as carrying more kudos or status than the next.

Atlantean architecture was based on the circle and the octagon, sharp angles being considered inharmonious to the human spirit. All dwelling houses (in the Age of Virgo in particular) were, therefore, round. So powerful was this circular influence that it lasted until the very latter days and was copied in Neolithic times in stone by both Atlantean survivors who managed to find safe havens in more primitive lands following the Flood, and visitors

to Atlantis from foreign lands who had taken note of what they
saw and endeavoured to replicate it. In Virgoan times the Great
Temple of Chalidocean was built on octagonal lines.

The Secrets of the Quasi-Crystal

In the sacred geometry of the Old Atlantean priesthood, numbers
in particular were seen to represent certain principles. The number
5, for example, was associated with the natural time 'sequence'
between Chaos and Order. This was seen as manifest in the quasi-
crystal which, unlike normal crystalline structures, is pentagonal
(five sided). You are probably bound to ask what is a quasi-crystal,
and why does it differ from our more familiar crystals that have
become so popular in recent years. There is rather a strange story
about this which concerns the reawakening of a personal memory
or, perhaps, the *open sesame* of a sleeping time-capsule in my own
mental programming. It occurred while I was writing my book
Time: The Ultimate Energy. I chanced upon the work of the British
mathematician, Roger Penrose, renowned for his study of black
holes and space-time singularities, as outlined by the eminent
physicist, Professor Paul Davies, in his fascinating book *The
Cosmic Blueprint*. Regarding quasi-crystals, Davies tells us:

> A normal crystal is a latticework of atoms arrayed in a highly regular
> pattern. The various crystalline forms can be classified using the
> mathematical theory of symmetry. For example, if the atoms occupy
> sites corresponding to the corners of a cube, the lattice has four-fold
> rotational symmetry because it would look the same if rotated by one-
> quarter of a revolution. The cube can be considered as the unit
> building block of the lattice, and one can envisage a space-filling
> collection of cubes fitting together snugly to form a macroscopic
> lattice.
>
>   The rules of geometry and the three-dimensionality of space place
> strong restrictions on the nature of crystal symmetries. A simple case
> that is ruled out is five-fold rotational symmetry. No crystalline
> substance can be five-fold symmetric. [1]

Translating this into the language of metaphysics, we may observe
the four-fold laws which apply specifically to this planet and the
frequency (time zone) in which it functions. Add the fifth
dimension and we enter the realms of timelessness, black holes,
dark matter or whatever names we may care to associate with these
phenomena which in metaphysics are represented in our galaxy
by the binary star Sirius. Needless to say, the major numbers to

which the Siriun energies resonate are 5, 7, 8 and 50, each of which featured dramatically in the symbology of both Mu and Atlantis. In other words, Siriun energies are the time-gateway through which all intelligent life in our part of the galaxy will eventually pass into the descending sine-wave of anti-matter. The numbers 5 and 4, therefore, represent the basic difference between earth magic and cosmic magic. The Atlanteans inherited the former from Mu, but added the latter once they had discovered the true nature of Time. This, like most of their other scientific achievements, was accomplished by a combination of left-brain hemisphere logical deduction and right-brain intuition, or far memory in the Atlanteans' case. I am inclined to go along with the belief that those spirits, entities or psyches that were responsible for the somatic changes that took place during the early years of the island continent's development were of Siriun origin, while the evolutionary quantum leap that allowed for their entry was orchestrated from the Siriun system.

The discovery of quasi-crystals constitutes in itself the opening of a time-capsule. It was in 1984 that scientists at the U.S. National Bureau of Standards (since renamed the National Engineering Laboratories) first discovered a strange material that appeared to possess a previously unidentified sort of order of the kind usually dismissed by scientists as impossible. How very metaphysical! This substance displayed the same type of order usually associated with a crystal except that its symmetries '*violate a fundamental theorem of crystallography: its atoms are arranged in a pattern that is physically impossible for any crystalline substance.*' It was, therefore, called a *quasi-crystal*. [2] As Davies points out, we have all seen walls tiled with squares, likewise hexagons (six-fold symmetry), as may be observed in any beehive. But there is no such thing as a wall tiled with pentagons because they simply do not fit together. However, Roger Penrose showed his fellow scientists that it was possible to tile the plane with five-fold symmetry using two shapes, a fat rhombus and a thin rhombus.

There are two forms of long-range order: translational and orientational, both of which are observed by conventional crystals with periodic lattices. Davies tells us: 'Penrose's tiling pattern, which serves as a model for quasi-crystals, possesses orientational but not translational order. It evades the theorem that precluded pentagonal symmetry because, unlike a crystal lattice, it is not periodic; however far the tiling is extended, no local pattern will ever recur cyclically.' [3] Normal crystalline development follows a repetitive pattern of self-organization, the physical forces acting on corresponding atoms in the different blocks being the same everywhere. But not so the quasi-crystal, as Davies explains:

> In a quasi-crystal each five-fold block sits in a slightly different environment, with a different pattern of forces. How do the atoms of the different elements conspire to aggregate in the right proportions and in the correct locations to retain orientational order over such long distances, when each atom is subject to different forces? There seems to be some sort of non-local organizing influence that is as yet a complete mystery. [4]

I have introduced the quasi-crystal at this point because so much information has appeared from various psychic sources regarding the employment of crystals in Atlantean science that it became necessary to effect a distinction between regular crystals and their quasi-cousins. Both had their uses in those times, although the true nature of the latter constituted one of the most guarded secrets of the higher orders of the priesthood because of their association with Time, the cosmos and, of course, Sirius.

The Crystals Cult

The use of crystals in Atlantis is probably the most commonly observed far memory or psychic impression. Crystal expert Ra Bonewicz tells us:

> Crystals were the most powerful single objects in use during the period of Atlantis. They were the principal source of energy and their powers were unsurpassed in healing. But, as with all tools of man, these powers and energies were also subject to misuse and it was the misuse of these very powers that caused the downfall of the Atlantean civilization. It was also at this time that many of the energies that focussed through crystals were withdrawn from Earth. [5]

The question naturally arises as to how crystals were employed in Atlantean science. It all depends on which period between the Age of Libra and the Age of Cancer (some 7,000 to 8,000 years approximately) one wishes to refer to. My own impressions will be limited to that period of Atlantean history with which I am personally familiar, which was during the reign of Helio Arcanophus. I shall also include some of the information he originally gave us, plus fragments of data collected from various reliable psychics and mystics with whom I have been privileged

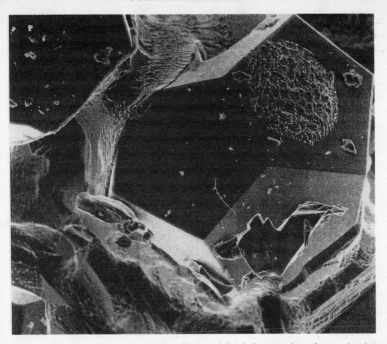

Figure 13. 'Quasicrystal can be distinguished from other forms by its unusual symmetry. The material can form grains in the shape of dodecahedrons, solids whose twelve faces are regular pentagons. The dodecahedral grain has fivefold symmetry, that is, when rotated by one fifth of a circle about an axis through one of the faces, its appearance is unchanged. The grain is composed of aluminium, copper and iron and is about 300 microns in diameter . . . Crystals can have only twofold, threefold, fourfold and sixfold symmetry. A crystal can never have, say, fivefold symmetry, because a single-unit cell that has fivefold symmetry such as a dodecahedron, cannot be assembled to completely fill space. There will always be gaps between the dodecahedral cells.' (*Scientific American*, April 1991, p.44. 'The Structure of Quasicrystals')

The metaphysical implications of this are as obvious as its shape, reminding us on the one hand that the material universe as we see it is not the only occupant of all-space, while hinting at the hidden subdivisions of Time on the other. In more recent times, crystals have been described as the braincells of Gaia, or Danuih to give her her Atlantean name, in which case I would like to propose that crystals with two-, three-, four- and six-fold symmetry as representing 'crystalization' and time-encapsulation would come under the influence of her left-brain hemisphere, whereas quasi-crystals could possibly be equated with her right-brain link with timelessness, the abstract, and her obvious intercosmic connections.

to work over the past forty years. No, I was *not* there during the latter days, so my only reference to this, and to other karmically unfamiliar times, will be the recollections of others, and what are generally referred to as The Akashic Records. I prefer to see this in terms of mental projection through Time to a point in Timelessness at which past, present and future exist simultaneously. Since none of us presently here on Earth can genuinely claim to be perfect, anomalies in interpretations of viewings from Akasha, Timelessness or whatever label we care to place upon the relevant facility, are bound to occur. Therefore, the best one can do in the circumstances is to acknowledge one's limitations and hope that one can place at least one small piece of the jigsaw into a position sufficiently appropriate to the whole to afford a clearer picture of what really took place in those far-gone days.

Edgar Cayce referred to a giant crystal known as *The Firestone*, which was set in the Great Temple in the Atlantean capital. This, he tells us, was the central power station for the whole country. The concentration of the sun's rays through this object's many prisms was of such tremendous intensity that it could be 'regenerated and transmitted throughout the land in visible beams similar to radio waves.'[6] According to Cayce, it was the misuse of this source of energy that eventually contributed to the final destruction of Atlantis. One more 'cause' to add to our ever-growing list! Cayce also referred to the use of crystals for the rejuvenation of the human body via the sun's rays.

Information concerning the use of solar power in Atlantis, along with lasers and laser power, sonics, and energy stored in crystals and released as and when necessary, appears consistent in most metaphysical teachings and far memories, although I have so far failed to observe any mention of quasi-crystals, possibly because their usage was exclusive to the secret orders of the priesthood that were concerned with the exploration of the nature of the cosmos via mental time travel, and communication with extraterrestrial sources. The mid-period (Age of Virgo) Atlanteans were also familiar with genetics, the personality types associated with each genetic pool, and the identification and isolation of those genes that carried specific E.T. memory banks. Such people were singled out for the priesthood of the Atlantean deity Ta-Khu, whom the Egyptians called Tehuti and the Greeks, Hermes. This Order carried the title 'Pursuants of the Arrow'. The arrow in question was, and still is, the Arrow of Time. Following the demise of Atlantis, many words and phrases associated with the old Atlantean knowledge of cosmology, quantum mechanics and astrophysics, were retained in the cosmogony and religious concepts of their colonies, the original meanings having been long-since forgotten. One example of this is to be found in the ancient Egyptian word for the Underworld – 'Tuat' or 'Duwat' (subatomic kingdoms to the Atlantean scientist-priests). There are many others, but since this constitutes a study in itself the best I can do at this point is to acknowledge the source.

Antediluvian Technology
Over the past few years there has been a veritable deluge of literature on the subject of technological achievements in prehistory, many of which carry E.T. overtones (or undertones) as the case may be. We have had flying machines in prehistoric India, portrayals of so-called space rockets and astronauts in ancient South and Central America, electric batteries from the Euphrates, as well as ancient computers and a host of allied phenomena, the authenticity of which is not germane to our present inquiry. What many people are bound to ask, however, are questions relevant to our world today such as: did the Atlanteans have a) air travel; b) space travel; c) atomic power; and, if the latter, did it in any way contribute to the final 'fall'? (Yet *another* proposed cause – their name is indeed legion!).

Let us start with a). One of the experts in this field of inquiry is undoubtedly Andrew Tomas, whose book *We are not the First* is packed with juicy morsels of information guaranteed to fire the imagination and test our tolerance to new ideas (or lack of same as the case may be). Tomas cites an illustration in the *Interplanetary Travel Encyclopaedia*, compiled by Professor N. A. Rynin of the Soviet Union, which depicts an Atlantean high priest being picked up by an aircraft against the background of a sinking continent. Tomas sees this rather extraordinary deviation from Rynin's normally rigid scientific approach as suggesting that, although the latter-day Atlanteans might well have mastered the technique of flight, the use of such vehicles was only available to the priesthood, and not in general public service. From the various myths and tales that have come down to us, however, it would seem highly likely that a form of powered flight was known to the Atlanteans from the Age of Leo onwards.

As for b), there are a large number of myths that refer to 'gods' having landed from 'the stars', bringing with them civilization, technological know-how, and a mystical teaching or gentleness and love. One cannot help wondering if at least some of these 'gods' were Atlantean priests and their families who had been psychically alerted to the forthcoming events and directed to the safety of certain places some time beforehand. Even in the days before their discovery of powered flight, the scientist-priests were alert to the possibility of interplanetary travel using the energized circuitry of Time. But did they ever actually use it? I do not feel qualified to answer this question, although it has been suggested by some psychics that it was seen only as a 'way in' that was employed in times of extreme crisis by those from whom the Atlanteans had originally derived the specific gene that had caused them to develop into the race they eventually became. This 'Time Causeway' is still open, and there are those who believe that when the next quantum leap occurs and Gaia culls her human flocks, their Siriun, and other E.T. ancestors, will utilize it to enter the Earth's timezone and provide a space-lift to some safe corner of the universe until conditions here have died down sufficiently to afford them security and adequate sustenance on their return. I do not claim to subscribe to this theory although experience has, however, taught me that open-mindedness is always a useful prerequisite to knowledge!

Now for c): did the ancients possess atomic weapons? The pundits hasten to tell us that all the signs are there. Tomas cites a case from Alexander Gorbovsky's *Riddles of Antiquity* where a human skeleton found in India was radioactive fifty times above normal readings. This led Tomas to wonder whether the Sanskrit *Mausola Purva* could possibly be history rather than legend, since it refers to an 'unknown weapon, an iron thunderbolt, a gigantic messenger of death that reduced to ashes the entire race of the Vrishnis and the Anhakas'. The corpses were so badly burned as to be unrecognizable, hair and nails fell out, pottery was shattered, birds turned white and foodstuffs were rendered inedible.[7] The *Samsaptakabadha* scripture of India also mentions airships powered by 'celestial forces' and describes a missile that contained the 'power of the universe', the power of its explosions being compared to 'ten thousand suns'.[8]

Although these and other cases cited are often taken as firm indications of the use of nuclear energy in prehistoric times, it could be argued that any of the phenomena described could equally apply to the descent and eventual intrusion into the earth's aura of some extraterrestrial object such as a comet, asteroid or giant meteor, since radioactivity can be generated by natural forces and is not exclusive to the suspect genius of *Homo sapiens*. One of the few scientists who have seen fit to comment on the accounts rendered in ancient myth and fable is Nobel prize-winner and pioneer nuclear physicist Professor Frederick Soddy. In 1909, when nuclear power was as yet undiscovered, Soddy wrote:

> Can we not read into them some justification for the belief that some former forgotten race of men attained not only to the knowledge we have so recently won, but also to the power that is not yet ours . . . it may be an echo from one of the many previous epochs in the unrecorded history of the world, of an age of men which have trod the road we are treading today . . . a race which could transmute matter would have little need to earn its bread by the sweat of its brow. Such a race could transform a desert continent, thaw the frozen poles, and make the whole world one smiling Garden of Eden. [9]

An Atlantean landscape pockmarked by giant nuclear reactors does not ring true, however, but perhaps we are talking fission rather than fusion. I do not doubt that the Atlanteans ultimately discovered a form of energy that was both easy to produce, free, and did not constitute an environmental eyesore. Would some metaphysically-inclined scientist *please* apply the right *open sesame* to the appropriate time-capsule and put us all out of our misery – or is that a privilege reserved for the post-tilt generation whom Gaia will deem worthy to inherit her body?

Technology in Atlantean Healing

The spiritual processes of Atlantean healing belong in a subsequent chapter, but there was also a more practical side to this priestly craft: that of surgery and bionics. It is well known that the ancient Egyptians were familiar with the practice of trepanning, but what other evidence do we have (from folklore, perhaps) that an advanced knowledge of surgery and anatomy was possessed in ancient times? The first hint I received of this was while I was studying the legends of ancient Ireland. The Irish mythological cycles tell how the Tuatha de Danaans, a 'magical' people who were 'wafted into the land on a magic cloud' in western Connaught, were engaged in combat with the Firbolgs. The Firbolgs (men of the bags) were led by their King, Mac Erc, and the leader of the Danaans was known as Nuada of the Silver Hand, who received his name following an incident in that very battle. His hand was severed during the affray, and one of the many

Danaan artificer/healers made a silver replacement which worked 'just like a normal hand'.

A corresponding legend is also found in the Arabian folk tale of a famous pre-Islamic rain god called Hobbal, whose missing arm was replaced by an equally functional gold limb. The Danaans were probably Atlanteans who made their way to Ireland via Spain and North Africa, as did many of the later Celtic tribes. Nuada's limb would not, of course, have been silver, but was more than likely a composite metal that was both sterile and untarnishable. I am inclined to believe that the Atlanteans did, indeed, possess bionic skills.

Ever Burning Lights

Stories of lamps that never went out are to be found among the legends of Egypt and South America, to be confirmed by travellers' tales in later times, although no-one, it would seem, has yet been able to retrieve one of these for analysis. For example, how did the ancient Egyptians manage to illuminate their tombs sufficiently to allow their artists to perform their intricate designs and figure work? Torches and lamps would have left their mark on the walls and ceilings but there is no evidence to support this. Researchers anxious to explore every possible logical answer have suggested that a series of mirrors might well have been employed, but surely any light subjected to such cavernous depths would have lost most of its radiance by the time it reached the bottom of the shaft, and would certainly not have been bright enough to allow for the execution of the kind of minute detail that many ancient tombs have evidenced.

According to my information, once the sun had turned her attention to other regions, the darkness was relieved by the blue-white light of solar-charged crystal torches, which could be turned on or off as required. This was achieved by moving a kind of 'shade' over them which immediately sealed in the power and closed off their brilliance. I seem to recall the lights looking very much like eyes, and the sealers like eyelids. What these 'lids' were made of I could not say, but they were very light, almost like a kind of plastic metal, with a silvery sheen, and they swivelled into position at the touch of a finger, but unlike our modern electric light bulbs they did not give off any heat, being cold to the touch. Whether these could be charged sufficiently to last for thousands of years I do not know. If such was the case, then the technology concerned probably belonged to a much later generation of Atlantean scientists.

Sonics

Back in the 1970s I was privileged to be taken to lunch by a former member of a Nobel Prize winning team, who confided in me that he was a confirmed believer in Atlantis. He actually recalled having been a scientist-priest in the Old Country during the Virgoan or mid-period and had been engaged in advanced work on sonics. I asked him why he had not pursued that line of scientific inquiry in this life, to which he replied, 'The world is not yet ready for it – when the time is right I shall return and bring my old knowledge with me.' Since he was elderly at the time, perhaps he will be reborn to take his place among the new generation of scientists who are sufficiently open minded to allow the seeds of past knowledge to blossom once more. After all, there is really nothing new in the universe, the sign-posts are already in position and it is only as we pass each one in turn that we begin to see in which direction we are travelling.

My learned friend had a clear recollection of the growth of sonic technology in Atlantis from the simple 'sonic gongs', each with its own 'striker' which was designed to resonate to different materials, to the more sophisticated ultra-sound devices used for purposes of communication among other things. For example, once the sonic keynote of a substance was confirmed, that substance could be homed in on sonically, no matter where it was buried or concealed, in much the same way that a metal detector is used today. However, Atlantean sonics covered an enormous range that encompassed both the ground beneath them and the sky above them. More I cannot tell you as I have never to my knowledge been a sonic scientist-priest. And without my learned friend to refer to, I must leave it to those readers who may well have studied this ancient Atlantean science to fill in the missing pieces. What both he and I did recall jointly, however, was the use of sound for sterilisation generally, and in medicine and surgery in particular. We also agreed that the Atlantean priest-scientists were familiar with the 'personal sonic or keynote' that is unique to every living thing, and that includes us. This sonic, however, is related to the eternal nature of the psyche and is not, therefore, synonymous with the personal genetic code which applies to the individual in one specific time zone (incarnation) only.

Cosmology

The High Temple at the capital city provided not only a place of worship, but also the equivalent to a well-equipped, modern university. Many Atlantologists, notably Spence, believe the Temple buildings to have housed an astronomical observatory equal to, or even in advance of anything we have today. 'Atlantis was the mother of stellar science', Spence tells us, and I see no reason to disagree with him. [10] It was surely Atlantean knowledge of the Siriun system that found its way into Dogon and Ammonite hands, while the astronomical records of the ancient Sumerians disclose a knowledge of twelve heavenly bodies in our solar system – Earth, Sun, Moon and *nine* planets, the tenth being a 'dark' planet that could not be observed because its specialized orbit was visible only once every 3,600 years. [11] Sparse remnants of other Atlantean astronomical knowledge also filtered through to the Chaldeans and other men and women of learning who followed in their wake, and it is only in recent years that much of this has started to make sense.

Endnotes

1. Davies, P. *The Cosmic Blueprint*, p.78.
2. Ibid. p.78.
3. Ibid. p.79.
4. Ibid. pp.78–9.
5. Bonewicz, R. *Cosmic Crystals*, p.95.
6. Robinson, L. *Edgar Cayce's The Story and Origin of the Destiny of Man*, p.59.
7. Tomas, A. *Atlantis: From Legend to Discovery*, p.40.
8. Ibid. p.40.
9. Ibid. p.76.
10. Spence, L. *The Occult Sciences in Atlantis*, p.33.
11. Berlitz, C. *Atlantis*, p.123.

8. THE ATLANTEAN RELIGION

The religion of the Old Country was structured into three tiers:

1. The secular State religion, designed primarily for the general public and those not specializing in priestly duties.
2. The metaphysically-structured doctrines that were taught to and observed by healers, sociologists, psychologists, and those mainly concerned with the humanities.
3. The higher, or hidden (occult) teachings that were reserved exclusively for certain branches of science and the senior orders of the priesthood.

The Solar State Religion

Let us commence with an analysis of the secular State religion, although I must once again emphasize that these impressions are orientated towards the Virgoan period rather than the earlier Mu-an (Libran) inheritance or the latter-day (Leo-Cancer) Poseidon worship and bull cults – if indeed there ever were such things. The State religion in mid-Atlantean times was a modified version of the old Mu-an solar code which had sustained a powerful injection of science and spiritual mysticism. Lunar worship was in no way evident in this period, which is confirmed in the teachings of Helio Arcanophus among other communicating entities. As there were no tides, the surrounding sea lapped gently around the eastern coastline, a profusion of foliage growing right down to the water's edge. So it would seem that the Preselenite myths were not without some foundation, and the Moon we see today, even if she had been around somewhere at the time, was certainly not visible *in her present form* in those far-gone days.

The Sun was not always accorded a masculine identity. For a long period during the Virgoan Age it was acknowledged as the goddess Heliona, although it was known that each heavenly body carried both masculine and feminine aspects, one or the other tending to predominate according to the prevailing influences of the Solar Age. The ancient Egyptians conceived of the Earth as masculine (Geb) and the sky as feminine (Nut), while the ancient Greeks, in contrast, nominated Zeus god of the skies and Gaia the Earth goddess. As we have already noted, the early lunar deities were all masculine: Thoth; Khonsu; Osiris; Sîn; and likewise the Greeks nominated a male deity, Poseidon, as god of the waters. Does this imply that the ancient water mysteries were male-orientated and not an exclusively feminine domain as some researchers would have us believe? Or are we being told that it is the males of our species who are predominantly emotion-orientated? I am not about to argue the rights and wrongs of either case, but it does strike me that there is some imbalance in today's world that involves an over-emphasis of the masculine principle at the expense of the finer feminine qualities of intuition, caring and continuity.

But to return to our Atlanteans: their State or Solar religion could possibly be equated with any of the State religions that have dominated our history to the present day. It was designed specifically to provide a devotional outlet for the general populace, while also according with certain cosmic principles concerned with the birth, growth and development of all intelligent life within our solar system. The Sun was the Mother and Father of Life, but it was not just the star itself to which the Atlanteans paid homage, but the intelligence behind that orb, known to them as a sublime Essence to whom they could address their prayers for help, healing, understanding, etc. The higher orders of the priesthood were only too aware of the true nature of the universe, but deemed such metaphysical information to be too much for the average person to cope with. The same can be said of today's world, where scientific discoveries of immense importance and illumination are eschewed by Fundamentalists who prefer to hold on to the contents of a book with which they feel safe, and which does not require them to think for themselves or stretch their imagination beyond its mental capabilities. Things don't really change, do they?

Telluric and Cosmic Energies in Religion

As the Atlanteans saw it, solar energies were there for everyone to see, use and feel. They fed the crystals that provided the populace with heat, light, energy, and many of the good things of life, and represented a manifestation of the god-force in everyday existence that could be touched, felt and appreciated by all.

Secular Sun-worship took place at each Temple, in the same way that services are carried out today in churches, chapels, mosques, temples and synagogues worldwide. There were also natural shrines, although the Atlanteans' advanced knowledge of feng-shui and earth forces usually meant that they built their places of worship on exactly the right spots, where the energies were in resonance with the Temple activities. For example, a healing temple would be erected on a spot where the telluric forces were conducive to rebalancing, and a place of learning in a location where the Earth's emissions were of the type and quality that stimulated the cerebral functions. However, this knowledge was not based on pure superstition, as it was understood scientifically that all life is influenced by subtle forces, both terrestrial and cosmic, which work via gravitational, strong and weak nuclear, electromagnetic and electrostatic fields. These, in turn, resonate with the elemental forces and the animal, vegetable and mineral kingdoms. Amongst humans their effect on both psyche and soma may be evidenced in such mechanisms as biological clocks and the psychological and physical disturbances that result from lunar influences and such phenomena as sun-spots.

In Atlantis, telluric energies were placed into two categories: outflowing and inflowing, or active and passive, also seen in elemental terms as fire and air for the former and water and earth for the latter. In later times, animal classifications were also accorded, the 'dragon' and serpent being two that have survived to this day. The addition of a 'fifth' energy indicated the extraterrestrial or cosmic influences which could overprogramme the aforementioned, thus altering their frequencies. Since all physical phenomena were known to be influenced by 'mind', the Atlantean priests were required to study not only the physical aspects of science but also the psychology of the intelligences via which those physical forces operated. It was as a result of this study that certain members of the Atlantean priesthood acquired their ability to 'commune with the gods' or, in more realistic terms, effect a telepathic communication with those intelligences that are responsible for the formation and evolution of the universe.

However, as any genuine student of the occult is well aware, one can only attain to those frequencies to which one's own psyche or higher self is attuned, in accordance with the magical Law of Equalities. So, while we may all pray to Isis, Freya, Thoth, Tara, the Atlantean deities or whoever, the extent to which that prayer will be answered, and the level at which it will reach the respective divinity, will accord with our personal stage of development. Try to move outside of this basic occult law and the fuses are likely to blow either mentally or physically, as many a 'dabbler' has found to his or her cost.

The Four Solar Festivals

The Atlantean year consisted of 360 days* and its calendar, which was later carried over into Egypt, was Sothic, based on the star Sirius. The higher grades of the mysteries were stellar, and Sirius orientated, but we will come to those shortly. First let us see in what kind of worship the ordinary people indulged. There were four great Seasonal Festivals, each of which was dedicated to a particular element, and although the Solar Deity, in either its masculine or feminine aspect, was the predominating influence, the other eight members of the Sacred Ogdoad were also represented. Bearing in mind that the island continent then lay in the southern hemisphere, the seasons and, consequently, the Four Great Festivals, were observed accordingly. It is tempting to try to tie these in with existing occult observances in Egyptian, Norse, Celtic or other magical traditions, but I must state that, although there may be an appearance of coincidence, the radical changes that occurred on the surface of Gaia following the Atlantean axis tilt must be taken into account.

The Festival of Fire This occurred in the middle of the first quarter of the Atlantean year when the sun was at its most powerful. Its tutelary deities were the goddesses Khiet-Sîn, and Philaeia. Its theme was Transformation. The celebrations for each of these Festivals always lasted for 8 days, and incorporated a public holiday which involved much feasting and merriment. Special rites were held at temples throughout the land; colours and symbols appropriate to the Sun, the element, and the tutelary deities being much in evidence.

The Festival of Air The second of the Great Festivals was

---

* Recent scientific research indicates that our bodies were originally programmed for a 25-hour day!

observed three months later. Its tutelary deity was the divine ancestor Ta-Khu, and its theme was Communication – with the cosmos and with the divinities. Celebrations for this Festival were usually held in high places, although in the plains areas where there were no hills or peaks, stepped pyramid-type structures were erected, and it was the custom for everyone to make the pilgrimage to the top to offer a specific 'gift' to the deities. These offerings were seldom of any material value and usually consisted of flowers, grain, hand-made artifacts and the like, which were then blessed by the priests and kept in the temples to be distributed later to anyone that might need them.

The Festival of Water followed three months later. Its tutelary divinity was the Divine Ancestor Khe-Ta and its theme was Creativity – in all forms. The principle rites of this Festival took place on the seashore, and people from all over the land would make the yearly pilgrimage to an appointed place at their nearest coastline to partake of the spiritual and physical refreshments provided by the State, and to display the results of the past year's creativity. Much dancing, singing and letting down of hair took place, as a result of which this Festival was usually the most popular among the ordinary people.

The Festival of Earth The last of these four festivals rounded up the Sacred Year. Its deities were Danuih and Akhantuih, and its theme was Unity – with the planet itself, with all other life forms that dwell thereon, and with the Cosmos as a whole. During this festival rites were held out of doors in sacred groves, stone circles, caves, and locations of telluric importance. Due thanks were paid and homage offered to the other life forms with which we share this planet, and to those elemental forces that kindly lend their particles so that we may have the physical forms through which to experience. This Festival was also known as 'The Time of the Children', and was much anticipated by youngsters the length and breadth of the island continent, who would parade in special masks and strange costumes not dissimilar to those adopted for present-day Halloween. These were known as 'the faces of Akhantuih', and legend had it that the originals rendered the wearer invisible!

The Religious Influence in Everyday Life – Priestly Sociology

Being a sacerdotally-ruled society, the religious influence naturally permeated throughout the whole of the Atlantean social structure. The priesthood ran the country along socialist lines in that the State took care of everyone; education, power, medical and welfare services and public utilities being completely free. Democracy as we know it was unheard of, however, but since the rulers were selected for their wisdom rather than their social status or public image, the populace had no cause for complaint while this practice continued. The Courts of Justice were held regularly, and anyone with a grievance was welcome to air it before the local high priest and his advisers. Trained animals were frequently used in these legal processes, notably lions and other members of the cat family, which were sacred to Khe-Ta and Khiet-Sîn, on account of their ability to read auras. This gift did not go unnoticed later by the Tibetans and Thais who learned it from their Mu-an ancestors, and, of course, the ancient Egyptians who observed it in their various animal-headed god-forms. Animals are frequently able to detect a lie much easier than we humans.

The Atlantean diet varied according to one's calling; members of the priesthood observing much stricter eating habits than those of less disciplined vocations. Red meat of any kind was prohibited, and domestic cattle and swine were unheard of until the latter days when they were imported from the mainland. There were many goats, however, who provided milk and its bi-products such as yogurt for general consumption. Sheep were kept purely for their wool, especially in the southern province where the weather favoured their comfort. Fish and bird meat was partaken by the ordinary people but amongst the priesthood these were forbidden and a vegetarian or, in some cases, vegan diet adhered to. Transgression of dietary laws constituted a legal offence, as did any act of aggression or cruelty towards an animal or plant. The kind of vandalism we see today, where animals are neglected and abandoned, and trees torn up by their roots by vandals or drunken revellers, would not have gone uncorrected. However, the people of those distant times were far gentler and more caring than their modern counterparts, so such offences seldom, if ever, occurred.

The exchange system was one of barter. Each zone yielded certain natural products which the other zones lacked. Fruit, for example, grew in abundance in the northern and central regions, whereas the south, where it was cooler, was the home of the smiths, metalworkers, engineers, and those employed in the heavier kind of work that is best suited to a cooler climate. A certain portion of all things grown, manufactured or created, was passed to the local temple. The remainder belonged to the individual to do with as he or she pleased. This meant it was bartered, and each town, city and village had its own barter market. Movement of goods between the zones was taken care of by the public utilities and mostly achieved via the complex system of waterways, both manmade and natural, that criss-crossed the continent. If, therefore, a fruit grower from the central province found that his annual crop was in excess of what he could barter locally once he had paid his tithes to the temple, he was at liberty to arrange for its transportation to a merchant in the south, who would negotiate its exchange for some more useful artifacts like pots or clothing. Public employees were also permitted to have 'sidelines', so although they received adequate compensation for their labours – and Atlantean working hours, being staggered, were far from long by our standards – they were at liberty to employ whatever skills they might possess in order to obtain any extras that might be acceptable. In summary, the necessities of life were provided free for everyone, but the individual could vary his or her standard of living according to personal output. However, sitting around all day doing nothing was considered an illness, indicative of a blockage or imbalance in the expression of the individual creative potential which called for the skills of a specialist branch of the Healing Faculty (psychologists and counsellors in present-day parlance). Besides, all fit individuals between the ages of 18 and 50 (excluding members of the priesthood) were obliged to make some contribution to the State coffers. Hobbies were, however, considered to be highly creative, and taken as 'activities' in themselves, so as long as one was spending a reasonable amount of time doing *something* constructive, and meeting one's temple dues, one could easily keep on the right side of the law.

Colour was highly significant in Atlantean society. In addition to the individual social statement aspect, it could also indicate one's position in life, specific calling, and contribution to society. In the priesthood it was of great importance, a priest or priestess's rank and specialization being easily distinguished by his or her apparel. I shall, however, be dealing specifically with the priesthood in a subsequent chapter.

Education was provided free to all, teachers being temple-trained. There was, however, a strict process by which children were, from an early age, gently directed into those avenues of expression to which their stage of spiritual maturity and accompanying talents were deemed to be best suited. This decision was, of course, made at the previously mentioned

Rite of Judgement (see page 100).

Just as the services of the healer priests were readily available at the time of birth, so did a particular Order of the priesthood officiate at the time of death. Since these highly trained men and women were gifted with etheric vision and skilled in the manipulation of the finer cosmic energies, they were able to guarantee the passing spirit a safe transition through the dark tunnel of timelessness into the world of light, and even direct it safely into a parallel universe or another time zone appropriate to its overall spiritual development. A physical body that had been vacated by its resident psyche at the moment of death was neither buried nor cremated but sonically disintegrated, this process being accompanied by a powerful rite in which the constituents of the body were returned, with thanks, to the four elements from which they had originally been borrowed. We are all aware of how, in the natural course of events, fire and air are the first to vacate the corpse, followed by water and finally earth, the latter usually involving a much longer period of time unless aided by cremation. The commands issued in this rite were therefore given in that order, accompanied by the appropriate sonics. This ancient Atlantean skill later degenerated into the *hekau*, or words of power observed in ancient Egypt, the true knowledge of which was long since forgotten. In the language of the physicist, the particles which had constituted the body were once again transformed into energy for cosmic recycling, in accordance with the Order-Chaos cycle that is natural to all things throughout the infinite universe.

An inevitable question is, did the Atlanteans have telephones, television, cars, and other impedimenta of modern society? The answer must be, no; not, at least, in the Atlantis with which I, and others I have worked with closely, are familiar. Messages from town to town could be relayed telepathically from the local temples, and in cases of emergency caused by accident or illness there was, in each small settlement, a sonic device that could be activated, that set up a resonance in the chambers of the duty healers. These signals were way above the frequencies that are heard by the human ear, although animals could usually hear them, which would often result in much howling among the resident pet population. This in itself was sufficient to alert the nearest healers as to an emergency.

An Atlantean National Health Service?

This brings us to the subject of healing for all. Since the methods and processes of Healing will be featured in Chapter 10, my comments here will be confined to the patient aspect rather than that of the practitioner. Every city, town and village was provided with an excellent 24-hour Health Service. This operated in a manner not dissimilar to the local General Practitioner/Specialist model currently in use in the UK, leaving aside the private sector. When a call went out for medical help, a Diagnostic Healer would be the first on the scene. He or she would assess the injuries or nature of the symptoms, using a combination of empirical medical training and etheric sight. If treatment could be delivered on the spot, then all well and good. If not, the Healer would send out another sonic call, this time at a different frequency, which alerted the specific priest or priestess to the nature of the complaint and the necessity for their specialization. According to Atlantean Healing methods, a specialized operating theatre was not a prerequisite for surgery, as sterilization was effected by sonic and mental, or 'magical' (occult) means.

So by what means did these people convey their sick or wounded to the temple hospitals? Since the Atlanteans did not have the petrol engine during the mid-period, transport was mostly horse-drawn, albeit well appointed and extremely comfortable, although according to some sensitives the latter days saw the advent of small, airborne carriages that were driven by crystal batteries. Plato makes no mention of this, however, which causes me to question its veracity, since it must have surely presented something of a phenomenon to the Egyptian priests who recorded the episodes that were subsequently related to the youthful Critias. However, there is always the possibility that it was included in the original texts, but suffered (or was deliberately omitted) in translation, the scribes of the later period being incapable of understanding its meaning. We will, therefore, give it the benefit of the doubt, along with latter-day aircraft and allied transport phenomena.

Certain members of the priesthood were able to practise both bi-location and physical projection, notably the High Priests, who had mastered a method of mental control over the molecules of their bodies that enabled them to achieve a feat similar to the transformer-room technique of *Star-Trek* fame. If this sounds too much like science fiction, then I can only suggest that my reader compares modern space-flight with the transport of a century or so ago, when anyone even vaguely suggesting the possibility of non-horse-powered vehicles was seen as a likely candidate for the local duck-pond! Besides, there is really nothing new under the sun, as the saying goes. We simply move forwards, sometimes backwards, or full circle through different, stationary time-bands until we have learned those lessons appropriate to our evolutionary development and ultimate spiritual individuation.

The Deities of Atlantean Religion and Magic

The Atlantean religion and its accompanying ethos is often referred to as being monotheistic on account of the emphasis placed on its solar worship in earlier times, and sea worship (the Cult of Poseidon?) in the latter days. This was not strictly true, however, for although the priesthood acknowledged One Single Creative Source, or point in time at which all energies and frequencies converged, they saw this Source as having many manifestations, some of which were more applicable to the frequencies of this solar system and our Earth than others. These manifestations could possible be equated with the Neters of the early Egyptian religion, who represented certain Cosmic Principles or basic archetypes. Animism also played a major role in the old faith of Atlantis, although as far as this belief is concerned, the citizens of the Old Country have some allies in today's world. For example, Dr Rupert Sheldrake's 'morphic resonance' concept acknowledges the existence of invisible energies that 'shape a growing animal or plant' and are able to effect communication through space and time; Dr Lyall Watson says it all in his book *The Nature of Things*; and Dr Evan Harris Walker believes space to be inhabited by an unlimited number of interconnected conscious entities responsible for the detailed workings of the universe ('Consciousness', he tells us, 'is everywhere').

One of the choices I have had to make in creating rites for this book was whether to try to recall the original Atlantean god-names, or to use equivalents from other pantheons. Donnelly was of the opinion that the Greek gods were nothing more than Atlantean settlers who apportioned the lands between them either prior to or directly after the Flood, while Spence had recourse to historical sources for what he believed to be Atlantean names, most of which originated from Egyptian, Chaldean or Greek sources. After much meditation and many requests for guidance, I came to the conclusion that bringing in familiar nomenclatures from other pantheons would tend to mar the pristine nature of the original Atlantean energies. Therefore, while I cannot guarantee the complete accuracy of my personal interpretations, I will try my best to present a suitable pantheon for the student who would like to worship, or practise magically via this ancient path. The following deities constituted the original Sacred Ogdoad of Atlantis, the octagonal recesses in the Great High Temple being dedicated to each of them:

HELIO
Male aspect of the solar deity
Sacred stone – white diamond
Colour – pale gold
Attribute (and totem animal) – Winged Disk (Falcon)
Correspondences – all male solar deities

HELIONA
Female aspect of the solar deity
Sacred stone – blue diamond
Colour – azure blue
Attribute (and totem animal) – Uraeus (Serpent)
Correspondences – all female solar deities

TA-KHU (Pronounced Tar-Koo)
One of the two Divine ancestors, believed by the Atlanteans to have
    descended to Earth from the Sirius system
Lord of Time and Space
Sacred stone – amethyst
Colour – amethyst
Attribute (and totem animal) – Caduceus (Dolphin)
Correspondences – Thoth/Tehuti, Hermes

KHE-TA (Pronounced Kay-Tar)
Divine ancestor, Consort of Ta-Khu
Feline divinity of sacred music, art, poetry and dance
Sacred stone – aquamarine
Colour – turquoise
Attribute (and totem animal) – Sistrum (Cat)
Correspondences – Bast, Artemis, Freya

KHIET-SÎN (Pronounced Khee-et Sheen)
Leonine goddess of protection and retribution

Dispenser of Cosmic Justice
Sacred stone – ruby
Colour – orange
Attributes (and totem animal) – flaming orb, exhibiting two separate flames, one orange and one blue, denoting dissolution/fission and coalescence/fusion respectively. (Lioness)
Correspondences – Sekhmet, Tefnut, Ashtoreth

DANUIH (Pronounced Da-noo-ee)
Earth goddess
Patroness of children, giver of spiritual and physical nourishment
Sacred stone – emerald
Colour – jade or mid-green
Attributes (and totem animal) – tree and equidistant cross (Horse)
Correspondences – Gaia, Isis, Dana

PHILAEIA (Pronounced Phil-ay-ee-ar)
Goddess of wisdom, philosophy, science and architecture
Sacred stone – sapphire
Colour – royal blue
Attribute (and totem animal) – masonic compass (Parrot)
Correspondences – Athene, Seshat, Minerva

AKHANTUIH (Pronounced Ar-khan-too-ee)
Negotiator of Chaos and alien energy fields
Sacred stone – topaz
Colour – clear yellow
Attributes (and totem animal) – crystal torch: blue-white light (Black panther)
Correspondence – Anubis

The correspondences given here are by no means exact, but there are certain similarities in the energies of the later divinities. Note the male/female, or passive/active emphasis, the ratio being five to three in favour of the former. During the latter days there was, however, a swing in the opposite direction. Of these eight deities, Helio, Heliona, Ta-Khu, Khe-Ta and Danuih carried specific healing energies. The Orders of the priesthood were naturally dedicated to the deity whose energies were compatible with the requirements of their particular calling. Thus an architect or a sonics expert would be a priest or priestess of Philaeia and a psychologist or anaesthetist would serve under the banner of Akhantuih.

One point that should be made quite clear, however, is the Atlantean concept of the Creative Source commonly referred to as 'God'. This they conceived of as embracing both Chaos and Order, the successful negotiation of these two aspects of experience being seen as an essential prerequisite to the forward progress of evolution, as our handling of the Chaotic aspects of the Creative or God Energies in particular go a long way towards making us the people we are. This doctrine of dualism later surfaced in the archaic beliefs of some of the surviving Atlantean colonies, and may be evidenced in its microcosmic/macrocosmic context in the phenomena of quantum mechanics and cosmology.

The Rites of the Atlantean Solar Religion
Many lesser rites were practised within this ancient faith in addition to those of the Four Great Festivals and the aforementioned rite of passage. There were rituals of Union (marriage); of coming of age (which was 18 years in those times); of Judgement (usually attended by all members of the child's family); various rites of worship, devotion, thanksgiving, and many others aside from the initiatory rituals undergone by those entering the priesthood. The three main daily rites observed at every temple throughout the land were the 'Dance of the Rising Sun', 'Hymn to the High Sun' and 'Prayer to the Setting Sun'. These were each performed in ritual song and dance by the priests and priestesses of the Guild of Musicians (those who associate temple dancing with nubile maidens only, please note) the movements of which told the tale of the birth of the Sun and her children, the planets (of which the Atlanteans counted 12, see Chapter 9), and the eventual demise of the star at which point its resident Intelligence would be freed of the worlds of matter to pursue its spiritual path through the finer frequencies of Outer Time. Since Atlantean music involved the quarter-tone scale it would be impossible for me to record these as they were originally sung, the human voice in those times being accustomed to coping with a different set of sounds from those usually encountered today. There are, however, a few pieces of music that many mystics and psychics see as bearing some resemblance to the sounds of the Old Country, notably the Vaughan-Williams *Fantasia on a theme by Tallis*, which might give the listener some idea of the kind of intervals involved. The same also applies to the dance movements. I have, therefore, decided to present simplified forms of these three rites that are completely safe, and suitable for those who feel

strongly drawn to the Old Country, but do not wish to venture too deeply into the magical aspects of Atlantean ritual which *do* tend to open up the psyche to a universe beset with both enlightenment *and danger*.

DANCE OF THE RISING SUN

To be performed at sunrise, facing due east. This was not, of course, the position in which the sun rose in Atlantean times, but as it is our star to which our Rite is addressed, it is essential that the present points of the compass are duly observed. The solar divinity may be addressed in either its male or female aspect – Helio or Heliona. Appropriate body movements may be added to these three rites, but care should be taken to ensure that these are related to the higher chakras, and that the energies are NOT drawn down for selfish ends.

1. Kneel down, placing your forehead, and the palms of both hands, firmly on the ground. While in this position inhale and exhale deeply 6 times. On the 7th breath, start to raise your hands and forehead slowly from the ground, at the same time visualizing a red-gold sun slowly appearing over the horizon. If the weather is fine and the sky clear, you will be able to observe this physically but, if not, the mental picture will suffice.

2. Bring up your hands slowly, making sure you keep your palms flat and reaching forwards toward the rising sun. (Although these invocations may be silently observed, they are guaranteed to be more effective if spoken aloud.)

INVOCATION

GREAT STAR, WHO IS MOTHER (FATHER) TO THE EARTH UPON WHICH I STAND AND TO ALL CREATURES WITHIN THE ORBIT OF YOUR EMBRACING RAYS I GREET YOUR RISING! AS THE FLOWER LIFTS ITS HEAD AND OPENS ITS PETALS TO THE GLORY OF YOUR MAJESTY, SO I OPEN MY BODY AND HEART TO THE WARMTH OF YOUR EMBRACE, AND HUMBLY REQUEST THE BENEFIT AND WISDOM OF YOUR PARENTHOOD.

3. Slowly alter the positions of your hands until the palms are facing upwards, at the same time tilting your head slightly

backwards. Arch your body for comfort, and also to ensure that you do not lose balance. Take four deep breaths and say:

HELP US, THE CHILDREN OF THIS SAD PLANET THAT IS YOUR CHILD, TO UNDERSTAND AND RESPECT THE CARE AND SUSTENANCE SHE OFFERS US. IN YOUR KINDLY RAYS, BESTOW UPON US YOUR HEALTH-GIVING ENERGIES, AND SPIRITUAL ENLIGHTENMENT SO THAT BEFORE YOU LEAVE US THIS NIGHT, WE MAY GAIN IN WISDOM, AND DISPENSE CARING, SPIRITUAL LOVE.

Pause for a moment and feel the sun's response to your prayer, for indeed you will. Then slowly lower your arms and cross them over your chest as though you were holding the Pharaonic Crook and Flail depicted in Egyptian paintings, and gently bow your head. These gestures signify self-discipline and control of the physical and spiritual bodies, while also humbly acknowledging one's minute role in the cosmic scheme of things. Repeat the closing prayer:

THANKSGIVING

THANK YOU, GREAT STAR, FOR THE BLESSINGS OF LIFE THAT YOU SO GENEROUSLY BESTOW UPON US, AND FOR ALLOWING US TO EXPERIENCE THROUGH THE WORLDS OF MATTER. FOR WITHOUT YOUR RAYS THERE WOULD BE NO LIGHT, NO WARMTH, NO EARTH, AND NO US.

End the rite with a personal affirmation of devotion, thanks and love, in your own words. Finally, visualize your whole body enveloped in the golden rays of the sun; feel its loving warmth, and slowly return to the kneeling position in which you started with your head and hands placed firmly on the ground.

This is important – 'ground' or earth the solar rays by allowing them to pulse through your own body into the Earth and you will find that Danuih partakes of their essence, adds her own energies, and returns them to you with her thanks and blessing. (This was known in the Old Country as 'Bringing Down the Sun'.)

FINI

HYMN TO THE HIGH SUN

An upstanding stance is assumed for this Rite, which should begin with the head bowed and hands crossed on the chest. While in this position breathe as instructed for No.1 in the first Rite, but on the seventh breath, fling your arms wide open and tilt back your head in a single, rhythmic movement, so that you are facing into the high sun. If there is no cloud about you will, of course, need to keep your eyes firmly closed.

INVOCATION

LIGHT OF LIGHTS, WARMER OF THE BODIES AND SPIRITS OF ALL LIVING CREATURES, RULER OF THE PULSATING HEARTS THAT THROB WITHIN US ALL, NOW THAT YOUR RAYS ARE AT THEIR MOST POWERFUL, STRENGTHEN US WITH YOUR LIFE-GIVING ENERGIES, AND GENERATE THE LIFE-FORCE THROUGHOUT OUR OWN WORLD AND ALL OTHER PLACES THAT ARE CAST TO YOUR CARE.

This invocation should be followed by a short meditation on the warming energies of the sun and how they permeate and sustain all life forms. The healing and life-giving aspects of the solar rays should also be considered. The arms may be lowered and the head bowed for this procedure, and a kneeling posture is recommended.

AFFIRMATION

IN RETURN FOR YOUR BOUNTY I OFFER MYSELF IN YOUR SERVICE, TO BRING THE LIFE-GIVING RAYS OF LIGHT AND LOVE TO THE HEARTS AND MINDS OF MANKIND AND ALL OTHER LIVING CREATURES; TO OFFER HELP, CARE AND HEALING WITHIN THE LIMITATIONS OF MY OWN TALENTS; TO LOVE AND RESPECT YOUR CHILD, DANUIH, AND TO SUSTAIN THE FIRES OF SPIRITUAL LOVE AND LIGHT IN MY OWN BODY, MIND AND SPIRIT.

Stand erect once more with arms raised and head back, and imagine yourself enveloped in the warm, embracing rays of our star-sun. Offer thanks with deep sincerity and in your own, special way. Then return to the kneeling position and earth the solar energies in exactly the same way as for the morning rite.

FINI

PRAYER TO THE SETTING SUN

This rite should be observed just as the sun is setting low on the horizon. Assume the kneeling position, facing due west, but with the arms forward and palms facing upwards as though open to receive a gift.

PRAYER OF THANKS AND NEGATIVE CONFESSION

I THANK YOU, O LADY (LORD) OF LIGHT, FOR YOUR BLESSINGS THIS DAY. THESE ARE THE WAYS IN WHICH I HAVE KEPT MY WORD TO YOU AND USED YOUR ENERGIES TO HELP OTHERS OF THE EARTH'S CHILDREN DURING THE HOURS OF YOUR BOUNTY:

Repeat aloud the deeds of kindness, caring and love you have carried out in the name of the Star-Sun whose love and care you yourself have in turn requested. All energies bestowed from the subtle planes or higher frequencies should always be passed on. It is in this way that the magical Law of Non-Conservation is adhered to, while you will also find that they are returned to you with interest. This was one of the main principles of the old Atlantean Solar Religion – that one should never take without giving.

Now return to Position 1 of the morning Rite, head and palms of hands pressed firmly to the ground and repeat aloud:

GREAT LADY (LORD) OF LIGHT, WHO HAS DEIGNED TO SMILE OVER YOUR CREATION DURING THE HOURS OF DAY, I ASK THAT YOU PLACE A FIRM PROTECTION AROUND ME, AND ALL YOUR CHILDREN, SO THAT WE MAY ENDURE THE HOURS OF DARKNESS AND CHAOS UNTIL YOUR RETURN JOURNEY BRINGS YOU ONCE AGAIN INTO VIEW OVER THIS PART OF YOUR DOMAINS.

(Kiss the ground.*) IN KISSING THE GROUND I GIVE MY LOVE TO YOU THROUGH DANUIH SINCE I AM ABLE TO TOUCH AND FEEL HER AT THIS MATERIAL LEVEL.

Earth the solar energies as previously described, and in conclusion, assume the crossed arms position, and say:

I HEREWITH WITHDRAW TO THE WORLD OF MY OWN PEOPLE, BUT AWAIT YOUR JOYFUL RETURN AT DAWN, WITH LOVE IN MY HEART.

FINI.

These three Rites may be observed either solitarily or with a group. If the latter, the plurals are naturally substituted as appropriate ('we' for 'I' etc.).

* A crystal, gem, or rock may be used if this Rite is performed indoors.

9. MAGIC/OCCULTISM IN ATLANTIS

The terms 'magic' and 'occultism' are guaranteed to strike fear into the hearts of many a superstitious person whose concept of their meaning is based on those sensational articles that appear from time to time in certain sections of the Sunday press. Let us therefore get a few facts straight before we start our analysis of the Atlantean attitude towards this esoteric study. The word 'magic' itself derives from the words *Mog*, *Megh*, or *Magh*, which in the ancient languages of Pehlvi and Zend signify 'priest', 'wise', and 'excellent', and from the Chaldean *Maghdim*, meaning 'supreme wisdom or sacred philosophy'. Likewise, the word 'occult' means nothing more than 'hidden' and is used regularly in astronomy without anyone turning a hair! As for Satanism, since the Atlanteans did not believe in anything even vaguely resembling the Christian devil, they could not be accused of worshipping such an entity. And yet we hear talk of their magic becoming 'black' in the latter days, so in what context is this derogatory and inflammatory term applied?

Atlantean magical beliefs were based on scientific facts, but with the added dimension of metaphysics since they did not effect a distinction between the visible and invisible worlds or, in the language of quantum mechanics, the particle and the wave. They were, therefore, more than aware that the Order/Chaos system dominates all life throughout the universe, and that mankind was faced with a choice between these two extremes in the swing of the cosmic pendulum.

Being fully cognizant of the dangers involved, the Atlantean hierarchy strove to guide its charges along the Path of Order or Stability, for although Chaos is recognized as being eventually self-organizing, the suffering that results from setting the Chaotic Principle into motion may be evidenced throughout world history. When Chaos rules, those who lean towards Order are drawn unwillingly into the suffering mode, as in the case of a major war, while the effect of Chaos on the individual psychology is exemplified in the Greek myth of Dionysus on the one hand and the Egyptian Anubis on the other. In other words we can either fall victim to Chaos or pass through it in the observation mode.

The Atlanteans inherited a degree of Chaos from the Mu-ans, which is why they strove to isolate themselves from the mainstream of Mu-an religious influence that prevailed during the Age of Scorpio. Once their island continent had broken away from the mainland they were able to exercise a degree of exclusivity that enabled the priests to shepherd their flocks back to the stability of Order that was to predominate the Atlantean ethos throughout the latter part of the Libran Age, through the time of Virgo, to the early years of Leo. The Atlantean magic of which I am about to write is concerned with this period of stability, and I shall take particular care to ensure that the latter-day swing to the dark magic of Chaos does not enter into any of the rites or practices that I shall be relating. After all, the chaotic or stable elements in magical power are determined by one thing – intention – which has also been defined in the selfish-selfless context.

It should be remembered that the practice of magic proper in Atlantis was exclusive to the priesthood and, as such, was compartmentalized into the different priestly offices. These included healing of both the soma and psyche, the various branches of science, and Cosmic Magic which was mainly concerned with the balance between the Earth forces, the rest of the solar system and the seed star, Sirius. In all these practices a combination of mental disciplines and rituals were observed. Since there was no monetary system, and the needs of the populace were supplied free by the State, there was little call for the kind of mundane magic that flourished in post-Atlantean times, which was mainly concerned with love potions, temporal advantages, financial gain and so forth. The fact that the Atlanteans were so spiritually cocooned is often cited as a reason for their ultimate fall; why they proved such easy prey for the unscrupulous hordes who arrived from the other continental mainlands in latter times for the easy material pickings that were to be had on the island continent. By the time the Atlanteans did organize a military force it was too late. The rot had already set in and the division between the elite priesthood and those of its followers who chose to pursue the gentler path of knowledge and wisdom, and the pursuants of the new materialism that had invaded their midst, became too wide for reparation.

The ultimate aim of all magical and alchemical rites and practices should be spiritual transformation, born of the realization of the true and full mental powers that are the natural heritage of the human psyche incarnate within this frequency we call 'material existence'. The Atlantean priests were well aware of this, and it constituted one of the ends for which their magic was designed. But there were others. The acquisition of knowledge, via all avenues of science, was considered as much a spiritual study as meditation and elative or mystical experiences in multidimensional awareness. In fact, the ecstatic element in mysticism, and all emotionally orientated psycho-physical reactions were somewhat eschewed, as they were seen as giving a false impression of true cosmic reality. The same also applied to overt manifestations of psychic phenomena, which were deemed to be a form of imbalance. The subtle worlds had to be negotiated via the faculty of intuition tempered by reason, and while emotional expression was seen as a necessary human experience, its over-emphasis, especially in magical practices, was considered unsafe for both the user and any others concerned.

Magic has long been divided into 'high' and 'low' categories, the latter implying its use in the more mundane aspects of everyday life and the former its utilization in the spiritual quest, or what is often defined by metaphysicians as Theurgy, of which Ennemoser wrote:

Magic, of which Theurgy, as the science of the hidden arts, was the child, forming a communication between men and the world of spirits, consisted in the instinctive but still obscure consciousness of a direct looking into and working with, and a communion and (magical) connection with the world of spirits. In early ages men were as firmly convinced that the most perfect half, the real man, had originated in the world of spirits, and that he derived from it his vital energies, being as little able to sever himself from its influence as the boughs from the tree-stem, or the stem from its roots. According to this innate magical belief, we find in all nations and in all ages the most deep-rooted belief, or at least a conception of such a spiritual

relationship, and the desire of communicating with celestial beings
. . . In the very earliest ages, when man had but just left the hand
of nature, and still sat at the feet of the Creator, when the senses were
still imperfect . . . man then communicated directly with spirits.[1]

The spirits referred to above were not, however, originally
confined to the departed souls of deceased hominids, or Biblical
angels. The animism that constituted the basis of Atlantean magic
was of a cosmic nature and not, therefore, limited to this planet.
It was also more in the scientific/rational (as opposed to the
primitive/instinctive) context that is understood and commented
upon today by some of the scientists mentioned in the last chapter.
Spence's somewhat adverse comments on animism (see page 37,
The Occult Sciences in Atlantis) have fortunately been refuted by
modern science, although one remark he makes does remain valid
as far as Atlantean magic in particular is concerned. In
commenting on Lord Raglan's criticism of Sir James Frazer's
Animistic hypothesis, Spence quotes Raglan:

'A scientist is a man who is trying to find out something. The magician
is not trying to find out anything. He blindly performs rites he has
been taught to regard as essential.' Magical rites, he continues, as
performed all over the world, have much in common. Magic
resembles religion in the general form of its ritual and in certain other
features. 'The consideration of these facts has driven me to the
conclusion,' said Lord Raglan, 'that magic is the offspring of religion
. . . preserved in a decayed or fossilized form. . . . Magic is a system
not of ideas, but of actions.' Savages and illiterates cannot formulate
theories. 'The savage performs his rites simply because he has been
taught to.'[2]

Magic may well have sprung from some ancient religious systems,
but bearing in mind the scientific basis of Atlantean Magic, I am
more inclined to heed the words of lawyer and Cambridge Classics
scholar John Ivimy. He wrote, 'Classical historians traditionally
dismiss tales of magic as unworthy of scholarly attention, but to
us any mention of a witch's broomstick or a wizard's wand evokes
the smell of a scientist's laboratory.'[3]. On the other hand, the
mindless repetition of ritual for its own sake can be extremely
dangerous as any psychologist knows, especially if the participants
are totally unaware of the nature and quality of the energies they
are generating. The arguments involved here are, however, too
lengthy to merit inclusion in this book so those interested are
referred to *The Psychology of Ritual*.

Figure 14. The evolution of the equidistant cross, some variations of which are believed to date back to Atlantean or even Mu-an times.

Magical Symbology in Atlantis

The Atlantean priesthood was well aware of both the practical and subliminal effects of symbols which act as access keys to the subconscious. Certain symbols were, therefore, seen as relative to different aspects of existence. For example, the symbol of the Sacred Four featured in all preliminary rites, as it represented the grounding influence essential to all magical practices without which the practitioner handling incoming energies could suffer the mental equivalent of a blown fuse! The Atlanteans inherited this elemental knowledge from the old Motherland of Mu.

Churchward points out the great emphasis placed on the Four Great Primary Forces in the Naacal writings, in which they are described as having played a primary role in the religion of early man. These Sacred Four carried out the Seven Commands of the

One Creator, from which one may deduce that the numbers four, seven and one were sacred in Mu-an magic.[4] From the earliest historical magical references to the occult practices of today, the evocation of this Sacred Four, as represented by the elements of Fire, Air, Water and Earth constitutes an essential ingredient in all magical ritual practices. Their basic symbol was, of course, the equidistant cross, of which there were many variations (see page 135):

Hapgood assembled the following table as evidence for an ancient worldwide civilization that 'for a considerable time must have dominated much of the world in a very remote period'.[5]

Table 2

Gods of the Four Elements in Various Pantheons*

	FIRE	AIR	EARTH	WATER
EGYPT	Re	Shu	Geb, Gea	Nu, Nunu†
BABYLONIA	Girru	Anu	Enlil	Ea
HEBREW	Gabriel	Raphael	Raashiel	Rediyas
PHOENICIA	Ouranos	Aura	Gea	Ashera
PERSIA‡	Atar	Ahura Mazda	Ameretet	Anahita
INDIA	Agni	Yayu	Prithivi	Varuna
CHINA	Mu-King	How-Chu	Yen-Lo-Wang	Mo-Hi-Hai
JAPAN	Ama-Terashu	Amida	Ohonamochi	Susa-No O
IRAN‡	Asha; Atar Oeshma	Vohu Manah Oka Manah	Spenta Armati Bushyasta	Hauvatet Apaosha
NORSE	Thor	Tyr	Odin	Njord
INCA	Manco-Capac	Supay	Pachacamac	Viracocha
AZTEC	Ometecutli	Tezcatlipoca	Omeciuatl	Tlaloc
MAYAN	Kulkulcan	Bacabs	Voltan	Itzamna
SLAV	Swa	Byelun	Raj	Peroun
FINNS	Fire-Girl	Ukko	Ilmatar	Kul Uasa

* Prepared by the anthropology class at Keene State College.
† The gods of the four elements in Egypt were different in different periods.
‡ Persian and Iranian mythologies were not the same; in Iranian mythology the four gods of the elements have their opposites, representing the good and evil aspects.

The ancient Egyptians observed the four elemental forces in the forms of the Four Sons of Horus, who were also allocated rulership over the four cardinal points of the compass. I have, however, come across several variations of allocation as far as these godlings are concerned; Budge, Lamy, and Jung each

Figure 15. The Winged Disk, one of the most important metaphysical symbols in Atlantis, was probably inherited from Mu, since it also appears in ancient Naacal and Guatamalan artwork.

offering different suggestions as to which represented what. The ancient Egyptians could have inherited this concept from either Mu or Atlantis, and from the variations available one is tempted to consider it a mixture of both. Since this is hardly germane to the Atlantean connection, however, I shall refer those interested to my book *Ancient Egypt: The Sirius Connection*, which covers the subject in some detail.

All Atlantean magical rites were prefixed and concluded by evocations and thanksgivings to the Four Great Elemental Forces who serve the great Archons, without whose cooperation we would have no planet and no material universe through which to expand our cosmic consciousness and spiritual growth. Elemental symbology, therefore, featured strongly in both the Atlantean secular religion and all its magical rites. The Great High Temple in Chalidocean, which was octagonal in shape, was surmounted by an equidistant cross, as were many of the lesser temples around the country. Several of the symbols that were of ritual significance in Atlantean times have come down to us, notably the Ankh, Caduceus, Sacred Eye, Uraeus, Pyramid, Chalice, Winged Disk, Lotus, Sistrum and Tet (stylized tree), all of which are as potent today as they were in the Old Country, albeit at many levels, some of which have not, as yet, been rediscovered (see page 138).

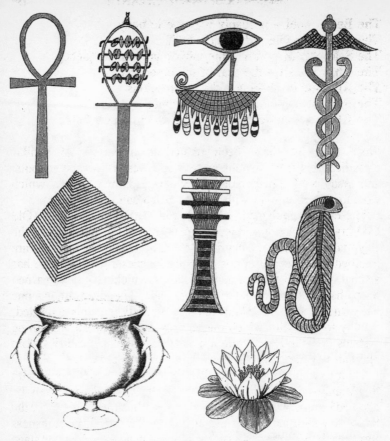

Figure 15a. Some Atlantean symbols that have survived until the present day (top left to bottom right: Ankh, Bast, Sacred Eye, Cacluceus, Pyramid, Tet, Uraeus, Chalice, Lotus).

The Subtle Bodies

The Atlanteans believed that it was possible to project one's consciousness beyond the realms of matter, into those subtle spheres that are designated 'hidden', and which encompass an infinite range of frequencies. This doctrine has also survived to the present day, with some rather strange variations. The ancient Egyptians, for example, conceived of the following series of subtle bodies:

The Sahu, or spiritual body – that which is abstract
The Khu, or spirit – the magical essence

The Ba, or soul – probably the etheric body
The Ka, or double – the astral body
The Sekhem, or power – the individual soul-frequency
The Ab, or heart – the seat of the emotions
The Khaibit, or shadow – the unconscious
The Ren, or name – the personal sonic
The Khat, or physical body – that which is perishable

Since then, we have been treated to a variety of similar classifications from various eastern and western arcane schools, and systems of transpersonal psychology, hardly any of which would seem to equate with the old Atlantean originals.

The closest equivalent I have found to the beliefs of the Old Country as far as this subject is concerned is the teachings of the Egyptian Ammonites. They state that although all living things are imbibed with a spark of cosmic consciousness, not everyone has a spirit, or a soul for that matter, both of which have to be earned in the hard school of material experience. Therefore, unless one has earned a soul, one's knowledge of other dimensions is limited, usually to that with which one is programmed by the prevailing systems of orthodoxy, while it is necessary to earn a spirit before one can negotiate certain levels of cosmic awareness.

Their meaning of the words 'soul' and 'spirit' equate more with the Atlantean originals in that these 'subtle bodies' could only be attained by a process of spiritual progress. In simple language, the extent to which any of us are able to project our consciousness into the subtle dimensions of the universe is governed by our stage of spiritual maturity, and likewise our ability to use our personal *Sekhem* and *Ren* as self-protectors. Therefore, if a group of people embarks on a guided meditation or path-working, the level of consciousness which each will attain will be designated by the speed and quality of their personal frequency. Dion Fortune referred to a 'ring-pass-not' which is not, as some might think, some pre-erected point in cosmic space which bars one's entry to the great beyond. It is actually the barrier created by what is commonly referred to as 'soul-age', but which I prefer to call a 'stage of cosmic maturity'.

The same occult principle is applied in the Atlantean magic of symbols. Let us take a simple example of the Egyptian symbol worn on the head of the Goddess Nephthys. This has been described by various authorities as, for example, a chalice, a basket, or a receiving device, while Nephthys herself is designated as both The Hidden One and The Revealer, the specific quality of her energies being associated with the Principle of Dispersion. The ancient Egyptians referred to the Khet-Khet, or Double Fire (the Fire of Solidification and the Fire of Dispersion), as being represented by the bipolar sisters Isis and Nephthys. It must have been far-memory, however, which once prompted me to use the Nephthian symbol to quell a riot and disperse a crowd from the comfort of my own home, which was some 30 miles or more from the scene of the event which I was watching on TV. In other words, the 'dispersion' aspect is not limited to any particular manifestation of the principle, and can be applied at any or all levels according to the Initiate's stage of awareness.

Translate the Nephthian headgear into the language of modern science and we get much closer to the Atlantean truth. The receptive symbol (bowl or chalice) represents entropy, that chaotic state into which all matter must eventually dissolve or descend and wherein its particles are dispersed to reform at another frequency, perhaps in a parallel or different universe. This brings a new meaning to the hidden and revelatory aspects of the Nephthian archetype, as the processes by which entropy reduces order to chaos are often 'concealed', in that the knowledge of its function and *modus operandi* constitutes part of a specific scientific study. However, when Nephthys does choose to reveal her secrets, the effect can often be mind-shattering. Consider the case of terminal illness when one is suddenly confronted by the medical fact that entropy has accelerated and the particles of which one's body is constituted are shortly due to enter the Nephthian Chamber of Dispersion to be reprocessed, via Chaos, ready for their solidification at a different frequency. Note that Anubis is the son of Nephthys by Osiris, and he alone is accorded safe passage through the Underworld, or to be more scientific the regions of Chaos, whilst still retaining his true identity.

So the myth is basically telling us that the principles represented by these archetypal characters, when united, produce a third force which can be utilized to negotiate the Chaotic Principle in safety. I am absolutely convinced that the family of Isis and Osiris were of Atlanto-Siriun origin, and that their story refers to several levels of consciousness, as well as to the cosmological history of both our own solar system and that of Sirius. In other words, the Atlantean priests clothed their scientific-cum-magical knowledge in simple parables that could be interpreted at any one of a number of levels. So, in the story of Anubis they are telling us that the psyche/spirit (call it what you will) can, if correctly schooled and suitably disciplined, negotiate Chaos without losing its identity and descending to Dionysian depths of depravity. But before it can achieve this distinction it must fully comprehend the nature of both Order and Chaos and, in so doing, lose all *fear of death*, accepting the onset of personal entropy as little more than a natural stage of transition in the never-ending cycle of birth and rebirth that prevails at all levels throughout the universe.

The Atlanteans understood that there is absolutely no difference whatsoever between humankind and any other life form throughout the universe; all are inevitably subject to the Khet-Khet, as the Egyptians chose to call it. However, in the persona of Anpu (Anubis – Akhantiuh to the Atlanteans) they did provide us with the necessary thread that would guide us through the labyrynthine caverns of Chaos to the regions of Isis beyond. The words of the Masonic 'Song of the Armed Men' from Mozart's opera *The Magic Flute* serve to show us how this ancient belief has survived to this day, via the mysteries of Freemasonry:

Who treads the path of Light that unto Wisdom leadeth,
He the purge of earth, air, fire and water needeth.
When him the awful fear of death no more shall fright,
Then may he rise to gain the sacred height.
Then with the enlightened shall he take his place,
To know the mystic rite of Isis, face to face! [6]

The 'rite' referred to is, of course, the Isian process of solidification following dispersion, which ensures the continuity and therefore the eternal nature of the soul.

The Magical Laws

What the Atlanteans understood as Magical Laws are more in keeping with modern scientific knowledge than medieval 'hocus pocus'. I have already outlined a few of these in earlier books, notably *Practical Celtic Magic* (pp. 218-21), but for those who have not studied this work I will list them again and add the additional precepts observed by the Atlantean priesthood:

The Law of Rebound
The Law of Three Requests

The Law of Challenge
The Law of Equalities
The Law of Balance or Equipoise
The Law of Summons
The Law of Polarities
The Law of Cause and Effect
The Law of Abundance (sometimes referred to as The Law of
    Opulence)

The Emerald Tables of Hermes have led students and researchers
to consider various other metaphysical 'Laws' such as the Law of
Contact or Contagion, which designates that things that have been
in contact with each other at some point continue to interact long
after separation. This ancient magical law was recently ratified in
the famous EPR Paradox (Einstein, Podolski and Rosen) which
was subsequently expressed mathematically in Dr J.S. Bell's
famous 'Theorem'. In more recent times, Professor David Bohm
submitted Bell's equation to laboratory tests and the theory was
confirmed. These experiments in turn gave rise to the idea of a
hidden or 'enfolded' universe in which all things are continually
interconnected according to some order, the nature of which is not
yet fully understood. Ours, and other physical worlds, real though
they seem to us, are simply material projections of some
unmanifest reality. At a certain universal frequency time, space,
matter and energy are inextricably linked in one hidden (occult)
universe. For those interested in the scientific aspects of magic I
have covered this subject in depth in my book *Time: The Ultimate
Energy*.

The point I am trying to emphasize here is that all this was fully
understood by the Atlantean priests, who treated it as 'occult'
because a) it was hidden in the sense that it was not observable
at the physical level, and b) not all the people committed to their
charge were capable of understanding it. After all, how many
people today can conceive of a series of parallel universes existing
simultaneously, in which every particle and wave is continually
recycled into what we refer to as 'eternity'? A large majority of
the populace still believes that there is no life after death, while
many refuse to admit to the fact that they even have a psyche or
soul. And yet the fundamental laws of physics designate that every
particle has a wave aspect, and although that particle may undergo
endless changes during the course of its existence prior to meeting
up with its antiparticle, whether in locality or non-locality, its

unmanifest wave aspect remains in contact with it throughout the whole process.

The reason why certain truths are 'occult' or hidden has nothing to do with members of an elite priesthood deliberately concealing them, but rather the inability of the rest of us to grasp them. Some scientists today reluctantly admit that the information resulting from their researches defies normal rationale; in other words it is metaphysical rather than physical. The younger generation, who have been fed a high mental diet of science fiction space-time travel, alien life forms, parallel universes, etc. do not, however, seem to experience the same difficulty as their parents in coming to terms with these phenomena. I share a view that is common among metaphysicians that we are returning full circle to the knowledge of Atlantean times, when science and magic were one and the same study, only this time the priests will be the white-coated scientists. But our wave aspects as well as our particle aspects also need food, and that sustenance is gained by spiritual or metaphysical observances. The Scriptures tell us 'Man cannot live by bread alone', meaning that unless we also attend to our metaphysical needs we are likely to suffer the kind of psychological fragmentation that often attends those who are beset by material stress but who have no transcendental belief to sustain them in times of crisis. This facet of the human psychology was well understood by the priesthood of the Old Country, which is why they instituted a complex system of Rites and Mental Exercises designed to effect the necessary balance between body, mind and spirit.

Astrology in Atlantis
The Atlanteans paid due deference to twelve planetary intelligences in our own solar system, while also acknowledging other stellar intelligences whose energies were relevant to the growth and evolution of all life on this planet. One is bound to ask why twelve planets were acknowledged when we know of only nine today. Astronomers are now aware, however, of a large body beyond the orbit of Pluto which has been named Persephone by some and Pan by others. Until science puts its final stamp on its presence we can take our choice, although I rather hope the astronomers will settle for the latter name. The eminent mathematician, physicist and cybernetics expert Dr C.A. Musès, writing in *The Lion Path* under the pseudonym 'Musaios', includes the two additional planets. He tells us:

Pan is the perturbationally indicated outermost planet of our solar system, with a perihelion just outside the aphelion of Pluto, that is, an orbit completely enclosing that of Pluto. Vulcan, already named by Neptune's discoverer, the great astronomer Leverrier, is the single infra-Mercurial planet in our solar system which was later denied by astronomers but which is shown to lie at a mean distance of 0.24 astronomical units (one such unit being the mean distance of Earth from the Sun) and to have a period of 43 days.[7]

This therefore gives us Vulcan, Mercury, Venus, Earth, Mars, Jupiter, Saturn, Uranus, Neptune, Pluto and Pan, which makes eleven. So what about the Atlantean number 12, and where does the Moon feature in all this, or doesn't she? The answer is that, in accordance with many of the myths, the Moon as we know it did not occupy its present position in the sky and was not therefore seen as a satellite as such but rather as a planet in its own right, with a male identity. Proof of this I cannot offer, and no doubt many psychics will have their own ideas about it all, but I am bound in honesty to present the picture according to the knowledge yielded up by various dependable psychics and channellers I have worked with over forty years. I shall be dealing with the pros and cons of information received via metaphysical sources in Chapter 11, however, when I hope to clear up a few salient points and avoid as much ego-knocking as possible.

Dr Musès also wrote at length on Sirius, its overall influence on Gaia, especially in relation to the anticipated quantum leap, and its significance as far as human affairs are concerned. Schwaller de Lubicz also sees Sirius as having some bearing on the climate of our planet and commented on the fact that climatological variation, if only a few degrees, can affect all life on Earth. In fact, Schwaller de Lubicz regards Sirius as being responsible not only for our own climate, but also that of the entire solar system.[8]

The ancient Egyptian Sothic calendar, which was based on the rising of Sirius, featured strongly in their early history. In studying this calendar, Schwaller de Lubicz came up with some very interesting facts:

The Sothic cycle is established on the coincidence every 1,460 years of the *vague year* of 365 days with the *Sothic* (or *Siriun*) *year* of 365¼ days. All civil acts were dated according to the vague year, composed of exactly 360 days plus the five epagomenal days consecrated to the *Neters*: Osiris, Isis, Seth, Nephthys and Horus.

The Siriun or *fixed year*, was established according to the heliacal rising of Sirius, yet the interval between two heliacal risings of Sirius corresponds neither to the tropical year, which is shorter, nor to the sidereal year, which is longer. For it is remarkable that *owing to the precession of the equinoxes, on the one hand, and the movement of Sirius on the other, the position of the sun with respect to Sirius is displaced in the same direction, almost exactly to the same extent.*

Calculations established by astronomers have demonstrated that between 4231 and 2231 BC, the approximate duration of the reign of the Bull *Hap*, the Siriun year was almost identical to our Julian year of 365¼ days. This period would cover the entire Ancient Empire, 'and we cannot but admire the greatness of a science capable of discovering such a coincidence because *Sirius is the only star among the 'fixed stars' which allows this cycle.* It can therefore be supposed that Sirius plays the role of a center for the circuit of our entire solar system.'[9]

De Lubicz also commented:

The double star of Sirius – which for Pharaonic Egypt played the role of central sun to our entire solar system – today suggests the existence of a cosmic system of atomic structure whose *nucleus* is this 'Great Provider,' the Sothis [*spd.t*] of the ancients. There might well be a need to revise our cosmology in the not-so-distant future.[10]

I am convinced that this calendar was inherited by the ancient Egyptians from the Atlanteans, who were more than aware of how all events on Earth are orchestrated from Sirius, the parent star of our own Sun and therefore the maternal grandmother of Gaia.

Atlantean Magical Rites
The Atlanteans are believed to have couched their magical knowledge in some secret language. Whether this is true or not, we cannot be sure, although we do know from Manetho (see Chapter 2, Endnote 14) that the language spoken by the pre-Flood Atlantean settlers in Egypt differed considerably from the native tongue of those parts. However, I am inclined to think that Manetho's reference alluded to the everyday Atlantean tongue, but I could be wrong. As I have already explained, Atlantean occult practices were divided into two classes: 1) those Ritual observances that were carried out by most branches of the priesthood, a few of which could also be handled by the layman, and 2) advanced mental exercises sometimes referred to in modern occult parlance as Mind Magic. The latter branch of Atlantean occultism was concerned with Stellar or Cosmic Magic, each

mini-rite or exercise being designed specifically for the individual
Initiate by the senior priest under whose tutelage he or she was
studying. In my book *Ancient Egypt: The Sirius Connection* I have
tried to capture the spirit of these exercises as applied to Siriun
or Sothic Magic, but I cannot, however, guarantee their
authenticity in relation to the Atlantean equivalents. However, I
am familiar with the formula the Atlantean system followed, and
the mental disciplines involved, which concentrated on the
balancing of the right and left hemispheres of the brain. The
following list of initiatory requirements may serve to give some
idea of the nature and scope of these exercises:

- A full comprehension of the principle 'as above, so below' as
  related to all the physical and metaphysical sciences.
- Recognition of one's Cosmic Roots.
- Facing, and coming to terms with the 'shadow' or 'id' (lower
  self).
- Negotiation of the regions of Chaos without contagion.
- The handling of multidimensional awareness without
  suffering psychological fragmentation.
- Externalization.
- Self-healing.
- Breaking free from this Solar System via the Solar Essence.
- The understanding and negotiation of the time-space
  continuum.
- Mental space-time travel.
- The recognition and identification of alien Essences and
  Intelligences in different parts of the visible and invisible
  Universes.
- The ability to change frequencies and 'shape-shift' either for
  self-protection, or to accommodate the Intelligences one is
  likely to encounter.
- The nature and work of the Archonic Kingdoms (Essences
  responsible for the formation, life cycles and eventual demises
  of Universes).

These are a few examples. There are many more.

Atlantean ritual magic is much easier to define in terms of set
formulae, however, and the two following Rites will give the
student some idea of the kind of pattern followed during the mid-
Atlantean period. The first of these is dedicated to Danuih, the
Earth Mother, and the second to Akhantuih the Protector.

AN ATLANTEAN RITE TO THE EARTH GODDESS, DANUIH

This safe and simple rite, dedicated to the goddess Danuih, does not constitute part of priestly ritual, although it was often practised by members of the priesthood. Small shrines and grottoes to Danuih were dotted about the countryside, and it was the custom for worshippers to leave gifts of food and drink for other travellers who might be too tired by their journey to seek sustenance elsewhere. Food was also left at such places for wild animals, who were also viewed as Danuih's children.

Rites to this deity usually encompassed requests for strength following illness; fertility, both personal and for any growing thing; help with the raising of children, and directions for housing relocation. Danuih also provided a stabilizing influence during periods of stress or anxiety. *In all Atlantean ritual, before any requests were offered, it was necessary to present a gift to the deity concerned, in keeping with the basic principle of the exchange of energies, nothing ever being taken for granted.*

The Rite would therefore begin with the preparation of a suitable gift for the goddess, which had to be something into which the supplicant had injected a fair amount of his or her personal energies. Last year's unwanted birthday or Christmas presents, or some piece tucked away in a bottom drawer that one has become bored with would not do at all. A baked cake, a carved wooden toy, a simple work of art, fruits of the earth resulting from labour in one's own garden, or even a thoroughly scrubbed floor would be acceptable.

Those taking part should be four in number or multiples thereof, although the best contacts are usually made when the Sacred Four is observed. (The Four Elements are ritually or verbally acknowledged). Ideally this rite should be performed out of doors beneath a canopy of trees, but taking into account the inclement weather to which we, in Britain, are often subjected, I am sure that the goddess would not mind if it is performed indoors, although a wooden floor would be preferable if possible. There should be a predominance of the colour green, and appropriate stones should be worn or displayed when possible. An equidistant cross should be marked out either in the earth itself, or by placing two branches of equal length one across the other to obtain the same effect. The participants, having first decided among themselves which of the elements they will each represent, may then assume their appropriate positions at each point (Earth/North, Fire/South, Air/East, Water/West).

The ceremony should be ritually opened by whichever member has elected to represent Fire. Each person must then evoke the presence and protection of his or her particular element, in the name of Danuih, whose overall protection is also requested. The four gifts are then placed at the centre of the cross by each person in turn in this order: Fire, Air, Water and Earth, accompanied by an appropriate acknowledgement of allegiance, love and thanks for her bounties. These simple prayers are best said from the heart, and it is not necessary to make them too formal, but for those among us who have not been touched by the Muse I would suggest something to this effect:

DEAREST DANUIH, WHOSE BODY IS MY HOME AND WHOSE ENERGIES SUSTAIN ME AT ALL TIMES, I THANK YOU FOR ALL THESE WONDERFUL GIFTS, AND ASK YOU IN RETURN TO ACCEPT THIS SMALL OFFERING WHICH IS IMBUED WITH SOME OF MY PERSONAL ENERGIES AND MY LOVE

Then place your hand on your heart for *four beats*, kiss the palm of your hand, and place it firmly on the ground, beside your gift, for four more heartbeats. You may then return to your position.

Once all the gifts have been placed, the requests may follow, but each must be prefaced by the words:

IF IT BE YOUR WILL

and concluded with:

IF IT BE MY DUE.

A short period of quiet devotion should then follow, in which the participants should concentrate more on giving than receiving, for as sure as Danuih receives, so will she give. This rite may be extended in length, but should never go on for too long. There will a point at which the energies will peak, after which the appropriate thanks should be given and the closedown effected. This is done by thanking the four elements and bidding them adieu, after which those taking part should kneel down and place the palms of their hands firmly on the earth while saying these words:

SINCE IT IS THIS DIMENSION OF DANUIH THAT MY
PRESENT CONSCIOUSNESS PERCEIVES, MAY MY BODY
AND SOUL STAY STABILIZED WITHIN HER EMBRACE
UNTIL SUCH TIMES AS I AM DESTINED TO TAKE MY
LEAVE OF HER, AND MAY HER ENERGIES MEANWHILE
PROTECT ME AGAINST THE FORCES OF CHAOS THAT
ARE MANIFEST ON HER BODY

This has a grounding effect and prevents any fragmentation of the psyche following the rite.

The ritual cross should then be well covered by earth, and never left for someone else to find and re-use.

RITE OF PROTECTION DEDICATED TO AKHANTUIH

This is a far more advanced Rite and as such should be treated with a high degree of magical respect. The number taking part should always be seven and never any more, although three is acceptable in an emergency. There should be a display of the colour yellow, and yellow candles should used, preferably in yellow or clear glass/crystal containers but no other light. A seven-pointed star should be marked out on the floor *prior to the entry of the participants*, who should form themselves into a line in the western corner of the room in which the rite is being held, as far away from the marked star as space permits. Care should be taken to observe the Law of Polarity by placing a male next to a female wherever possible, and when there is a preponderance of one particular sex, members should decide among themselves who will represent the active energies and who the passive energies. If there are more women taking part than men then a woman must assume the 'leader point', and conversely should there be more men than women.

The leader should be positioned at the end of the line. He or she should carry a staff and a lamp, torch or lighted candle, and the Rite should commence by the Leader striking the floor seven times, raising the lamp or candle, and motioning the first in line to proceed clockwise towards the apex of the seven-pointed star. From this point he/she (the first in line, that is) continues to move around until the Leader at the end of the line has reached the apex, each of the other participants assuming his or her appropriate positions at the vacant points.

The leader should then place his/her staff at a position pointing to the centre of the star, and acknowledge the Four Elements before raising the light above his/her head to invoke Akhantuih for protection against the fragmenting forces of Chaos. Each person present should then proceed as follows: place the palm of the right hand on the forehead, and the palm of the left hand on the back of the head. Repeat the following words:

MY SPIRIT CONTROLS MY MIND AND MY MIND CONTROLS MY BODY.

Now, cross the arms over the head so that the palm of the left hand is pressed against the right upper side of the head and vice versa with the left hand, linking both thumbs at the top. Drop the head slightly backwards and look upwards. Repeat the words:

MY LOGIC CONTROLS MY INTUITION AND MY INTUITION TEMPERS MY LOGIC. THUS, WITH THE GUIDANCE OF AKHANTUIH, I MAY PASS IN SAFETY THROUGH THE REGIONS OF CHAOS AND THE DARK PLACES OF FEAR, AND IN RETURN FOR THIS BLESSING I PROMISE TO GIVE AKHANTUIH SEVEN MINUTES OF MY DAY, TO BE SPENT IN MENTAL DISCIPLINE, PROGRAMMING, AND BALANCING THE TWO HEMISPHERES OF MY BRAIN.

The supplicant should remain in this position for the count of seven heartbeats, after which the hands may be lowered and the head bowed in acknowledgement of the divinity for seven more heartbeats. The seven minute 'gift of time' was usually carried out during the rite, but it can also be attended to prior to the ceremony, or at any time when the supplicant is able to snatch a few quiet moments. However, once the promise is made it *must be carried out within the 24 hours surrounding the performance of the Rite, or the Law of Rebound will automatically be activated.*

The Leader should then address a general prayer to Akhantuih for all-round protection, from natural causes, accidents, bad dreams and so forth, according to what has been decided by the participants before the commencement of the rite. Rites to Akhantuih were always performed prior to undergoing surgery, or in times of mental confusion, uncertainty and doubt.

The Leader should then move clockwise round the inside of the star, pausing before each point and raising his/her candle or torch above the head of the occupying participant. The following words should be said each time the light is raised:

HERE IS THE LIGHT OF REASON AND INTUITION. IT IS THE TORCH OF AKHANTUIH, AND AS SUCH IT WILL GUIDE YOU SAFELY THROUGH THE DAYS AND NIGHTS OF THE ENSUING MORROWS. TRAVEL SAFELY IN HIS NAME.

The Rite should be concluded by the Leader moving to the centre of the star and striking the ground seven times with his/her rod. The words to be repeated are:

I NOW DEEM ALL DOORS TO THE REALMS OF AKHANTUIH TO BE DULY CLOSED AND SEALED, NOT TO BE REOPENED WITHOUT HIS DIVINE, PROTECTIVE PRESENCE.

The leader then returns temporarily to his/her position at the apex, raises his torch/candle high and offers love and thanks to the deity for his presence and help, and to the Four Elements respectively. He/she then breaks the star formation by stepping backwards from his/her position, and proceeds clockwise to lead the others away from the formation. The seven-pointed star should then be dismantled, and the Akhantuian energies earthed by merriment and laughter.

Endnotes
1. Spence, L. *The Occult Sciences in Atlantis*, pp.42–3.
2. Ibid. p.38.
3. Ivimy, J. *The Sphinx And The Megaliths*, p.96.
4. Churchward, J. *The Lost Continent of Mu*, p.163.
5. Hapgood, C. *Maps of the Ancient Sea Kings*, p.202.
6. Mozart, W.A. (trs. E. Dent). *The Magic Flute*.
7. Musaios (Musès, C.A.). *The Lion Path*, p.60.
8. Hope, M. *Time: The Ultimate Energy*.
9. Schwaller de Lubicz, R.A. *Sacred Science*, pp.26–7.
10. Ibid. p.28.

10. THE PRIESTS OF ATLANTIS

The Atlantean priesthood was a highly structured organization in which the specific role played by all concerned designated their place in the sacerdotal hierarchy. Since the system of government in Atlantis was not democratic, priestly and administrative positions were not decided by public election but allotted according to a) the initial Judgement, and b) subsequent progress and skills developed during the maturing years. The practical administration of the country was run by the equivalent to our present-day civil service, under the direction of what were known as Administrators. Although these men and women were not priests themselves, they were ultimately answerable to the senior priests, both for the care of those in their employ, and the way in which their duties were carried out. Should any problems arise, however, there was always a priest available to advise them.

The priestly hierarchy was easily distinguishable to the general public by its apparel, each branch displaying specific symbols, colours and robes. So, just as we, today, are able to recognize an officer of the Law by his uniform, or a gentleman of the cloth by his collar, the Atlantean people knew whether the priest they were passing in the street was a Healer, Magi, first-year novitiate, and so forth, and would respond accordingly. During their leisure time, and while in the confines of their own family environment, however, members of the Atlantean priesthood could dress as they chose, although they were always obliged to wear at least one small badge of office such as an earring, pendant or headband, by which they could be recognized.

The Colours of the Priesthood

The use of colour featured strongly in the Atlantean ethos, and Plato's description of the blue and white robes of the Atlantean priests evidence the fact that this tradition was carried right through to the latter days, blue, white and gold being the sacred colours of the Atlantean priesthood. The basic garment of the Higher Orders was always white, that of the middle Orders was light blue, and the Junior Orders wore pale green. Particular callings were indicated by the colour of the belts or sashes, although the plain, azure sash was worn by High Priests only. Thus, a priest garbed in a white tunic with an orange sash would be a senior occultist specializing in exorcism, and one whose basic robe was pale green caught in at the waist with a royal blue sash would be a novitiate or student scientist. Dual-coloured sashes were only worn by the Priests and priestesses of the Order of Passage, to denote the nature of their specific tasks. But there were also other emblems and significators of rank and purpose; precious and semi-precious stones and metals, for example, featured impressively in the priestly ranking system. Headbands were worn by all members of the priesthood during the course of their duties. A silver coloured band worn by a Healer denoted a speciality in mental or psychological healing, while an orichalcum band stood for expertise in the field of physical medicine or surgery. The headbands worn by the lesser ranks were usually plain, jewels or specific symbols being displayed only by those of the higher echelons or advanced qualification.

Each town had its temple, and in every temple there was a local High Priest and his attendant staff. When officiating at their temples these High Priests wore a special kind of headdress which was not dissimilar to that worn by the Pharaohs in ancient Egypt. The headband of rank, which featured a precious stone in a raised position on the forehead, was worn over this, the colour of which would accord with the nature of the wearer's priestly calling. Each priest also wore a ring that displayed the stone appropriate to the deity in whose Order he or she had been ordained. Danuih, for example, was the patroness of nurses and teachers of the young, so a teacher or healer specializing in that branch of the healing arts would display an emerald or a green stone in his or her ring.

Garments of Initiation

During the long years of their studies, the Temple novitiates wore short cotton tunics, and simple sandals made from an artificially manufactured material, not dissimilar to some of the modern synthetics, that was exclusive to the Atlantis of the period. Although shoes and sandals made from goat-hide were often worn by the general populace this was not allowed in the priesthood. The goats used were not specially bred for this purpose, however, nor were they killed for their skins when young. Only when they had lived a full life, and old age was upon them, were they put quietly to sleep and their skins taken for footwear and other practical uses. However, whenever this was done a special rite was performed to the spirit of the goat, in which it was thanked for its many years of service and for the subsequent use of its skin.

Upon passing the final Initiation into the priesthood, the Initiate was presented with a pair of special, gold-coated sandals, which he or she was obliged to wear when carrying out the specific functions of his or her calling. At all other times members of the priesthood were at liberty to dress how they wished. Priests and priestesses were not obliged to live within the temple precincts once they had fulfilled their period of study and were fully qualified, and most of those who had accepted the Rite of Union (marriage) usually had homes in the countryside outside the city. All members of the priesthood were able to marry, although they inevitably chose mates from within their own calling for obvious reasons.

The Chief High Priest resided in the capital city where he or she officiated at both the regular secular or public rites of the Solar Religion, and the Inner or secret rites of the priesthood. The ceremonial regalia of the Chief High Priest was richly ornate by modern standards, and he or she always carried or displayed some special Symbol of Office when making public appearances. The most enduring of these metaphysical social statements was undoubtedly the high headdress or ceremonial crown, which featured a raised jewel-encrusted winged disk, set in gold. Another symbol was a huge blue-white diamond, worn suspended from a heavy gold chain, and many were the legends of its power and the miracles wrought through its energies.

Healing Methods in Atlantis

In the Atlantean medical profession, healers were divided into two main categories – those who specialized in healing the mind and those whose specialization was the soma or body. These two divisions were also subdivided, the former incorporating specialists in occult studies who undertook such functions as exorcism, which demanded a sound knowledge of physics and metaphysics. The Healers of the Body included surgeons, those skilled in physical manipulation, orthopaedic specialists and so forth. However, all healing was seen in the holistic context, so it was often necessary for two or three different types of healers to confer together over a patient. There were also Orders of priests and priestesses who specialized in the healing of animals, plants, and the Earth itself, being dedicated to the tutelary deities Khe-Ta, Khiet-Sîn, and Danuih respectively, although the Solar Healers were also able to apply their skills in those directions should the necessity arise. Khe-Ta was the patroness of domestic animals, and Khiet-Sîn of wild animals.

Illness was viewed as a manifestation of the Chaotic principle. There were obviously others. The forces of Order and Chaos, as represented by the entwining serpents of the Caduceus, needed to be kept in balance. When Chaos assumed the upper hand its energies could manifest in any of several illnesses which, if left uncorrected, could result in death. A preponderance of Order also had its side effects, however, since it was observed that those people who enjoyed continued good health suffered far more when Chaos ultimately caught up with them, which was mostly in later life. There would appear to be some truth in the old saying 'cracked crocks last the longest', the inference being that those of us who are beset with a series of niggling health problems for most of our lives, tend to take better care of our health and are therefore likely to spot any serious problems early enough to nip them in the bud!

In the Old Country healing was applied at three levels, the spiritual, the psychological and the somatic or physical. Even something as physical as breaking a leg was seen to have either psychological or karmic connotations, and treated accordingly with a combination of practical medicine, auric repair, and mental and spiritual counselling, the latter of which was carried out by those initiated into the Order of Passage. In a society that takes care of many of the kind of material worries and stresses that face us today, Chaos inevitably found other ways of tipping the scales in its favour, but that constitutes a study in itself and a hypothetical one at that since none of us really knows for sure what happened in those times, and even if we think we do, we are unable to offer any empirical evidence as to the authenticity of our observations.

The Orders of Passage

This branch of the Atlantean priesthood, which was a subsidiary of the Healing Orders, might prove of particular interest to modern counsellors and psychologists, since these practices fell within its field of jurisdiction. Priests and priestesses of this Order were responsible for all Rites of Passage. These included rites of birth, maturation, union, menopause (in both sexes) and the eventual passing of the spirit, and embraced what is often referred to among modern psychics as 'rescue work' in other dimensions. In the 'Final Rite', the officiating members of the Order were assisted by two sonic specialists, who attended to the disintegration of the physical shell. Also observed as rites of passage were seasonal rites, which were specially designed to adjust the pineal gland to the shortening or lengthening of the days as the case might be. Psychological counselling was effected at several levels, problems arising from experiences in other time-zones (former lives), for example, often proving the cause of mental maladjustments. It was also the duty of these priests/priestesses to guide their patients along their correct karmic path or pre-chosen destiny, which naturally called for astrological skills among other things. The Order of Passage worked in close conjunction with other branches of the Healing Orders, the connection between both functions being obvious.

The two colours featured in the sashes of this Order stood for the practical or earthy (sage green) and the 'feeling' aspect (soft rose pink), both of which were deemed essential qualities in those who practised within it. A high degree of psychic sensitivity was also essential. Akhantuih, Ta-Khu, and Danuih were the Order's deities; Akhantuih for his ability to negotiate Chaos, Ta-Khu as god of Healing and Time, and Danuih for the grounding necessary in the real world in which the particular fragment was experiencing. Priests and priestesses of the Orders of Passage always wore platinum headbands with either pink or pale green stones set in the front, the more senior among them displaying a bi-coloured tourmaline, a stone which is often found in contrasting bands of pale green and soft pink.

Priestly Training

Although training for the Atlantean priesthood commenced at a comparatively early age and the candidates were elected from childhood, they did not go straight from their primary studies into the Halls of Learning in the way that young people today tend to exchange their school desks for the hallowed halls of Academe. After completing a course of general education which could possibly be equated with the British GCSE, these Atlantean novices were required to leave home and travel round the provinces in the care of specialized educationalists under whose tutelage they learned to observe the ways, needs and day-to-day activities of the ordinary people. During this period, which was usually three years, they were obliged to undertake social and community work such as helping out in hospitals, looking after children, familiarizing themselves with agriculture, husbandry, and the needs of the animal and plant kingdoms. Only when this period was deemed to be satisfactorily completed, were they allowed to commence their specialized study or studies. Four years was the minimum period of training for a priest or priestess whose duties would be mainly religious and concerned with the administration and day-to-day activities of a local temple. For scientists, metaphysicians, certain branches of the healing profession and other more highly specialized fields the minimum study requirement was seven years, although for the discoverers, of course, their specialization constituted a lifetime study.

Terrestrial and Extraterrestrial Duties

The duties of the higher ranks of the Atlantean priesthood included responsibility for the health, balance, and well being of the planet Earth, which included such duties as affording Danuih protection against excessive sunspot activity and any other intrusive celestial phenomena, and keeping in regular communication with beneficent extraterrestrial intelligences, particularly from the region of Sirius. Since it was also realized that not all 'signs in the heavens' were necessarily of benign intent, a watchful eye was also kept on any unusual cosmic occurrence that might bode ill for the Earth and her denizens. It was this watchfulness that enabled the latter-day priests of Light to observe the ultimate fate of the island continent, and judge the retrogressive step that catastrophe was likely to have on the evolution of the Earth and all that dwelt thereon.

The Sirius Factor

There has so far been much talk of the influence of Sirius on Atlantean and, come to that, all earthly affairs. From where did the Atlanteans obtain this knowledge and how did they manage to ensure that it was perpetuated over the ensuing ages? Just as many people today are taught to believe that a manifestation of the Creative Force took on human form in Palestine at the commencement of the Piscean Age, while others view their Prophet as the divine representative on Earth, so the Atlanteans believed that they, too, had received a visit from 'above' in the persons of Ta-Khu and Khe-Ta, whom they venerated as the founders of their race. The only difference is that the Atlanteans knew from whence these divinities hailed, since their legends told them that they were not earth born but arrived in a shining sphere from a planet in the system of the binary star, Sirius – which adds a whole new dimension to our magical studies, that of the ET.

Many followers of the old gods and goddesses are reluctant to admit to any ET influence, seeing everything ancient in terms of archaic pagan faiths and their accompanying pantheistic and animistic beliefs. There is an answer to that, of course, which is that we only tend to 'remember' what we have actually experienced in other time-zones, or what we carry in the memory banks of our genes. There is, in fact, ample evidence in many ancient traditions to suggest some external intervention in the affairs of the children of Gaia, or Danuih if you wish to keep in the Atlantean idiom. The ancient Order of Egyptian Ammonites, for example, has retained to this day the legend of the arrival of Auset and Ausar (Isis and Osiris) from 'outer space' and, as I explained earlier, have observed a calendar that commenced with the appearance of these twin Neters, while the influence exerted on Egypt by the Sothic calendar with all that it implied can be read in any book on Egyptology. The custodians of this ancient faith were also familiar with the Siriun/Atlantean leonine deity Khiet-Sîn, whom they acknowledge in the name of Nebt Sekhmet Montu, which title is carried by the High Priestess of their Order to this day. Here is an extract from a letter I received from the Chief Scribe of the Ammonites in response to my enquiry regarding any information they might have concerning Sirius. This was originally reproduced, together with other Ammonite material, in *Ancient Egypt: The Sirius Connection*:

Known by us as the Star of the New Day (or year) and the commemorative star of the ascension of Our Lady (Isis) to the Lotus Throne of the Great House (LHS) a little over 10,450 years ago.

Known as The Star of Commemoration of the birth of the five great Neters (gods) upon the Mountain of Creation, Sinai Mountain in Sinai, Egypt namely: Us-Ar (Osiris), Auset (Isis), Setekh (Set), Nebt Het (Nephthys) and Heru (Horus). The star of the added on days of the Epact, which are five days for three years and six days on the fourth year.

Esoterically known as The Source from whence came the Neters from out of the Universe to our peoples, The Ammonites, and our cousins, the Tutsi peoples. The Tutsi people hold we the Ammonite peoples to be the Ones of the Shining Faces who left their footsteps on the mountains of stone by the tone uttered from their mouths, the Ones who created 'The Mountains' of perfection in the north and whose voice commanded the respect of God, who departed from us (the Tutsi), by moving to the east out of the beloved land soon to be ravaged by the savages (Arabs) of the lands to the east. The Ammonites wrote upon the rock of the mountain with fingers of fire, travelled upon the air without wings, moved rivers out of their sources by thought, and gifted us (the Tutsi) and our cousins (The Dogon) [sic.] with the gift of our origins and great magic. And when they left they caused great sorrow amongst our peoples (the Tutsi), some going east to the land of the mountains by the sea, some going back to the Source in the heavens where they say by mathematics the spiritual history of their world took place, as it did upon their land and our races of this world, and of which our cousins, The Dogons, know more, for we achieved to the side of Hekau 'Words that move', and they, the Dogons, to the matters of origin. And although our skins vary greatly we are one race, for we married and lived with these Shining Ones in our ancestral lands, for they prophesied the coming of the wild ones who shall cause the name of their leader the one of evil to be heard throughout the Holy Land as God Itself, but who in turn would succumb to the Shining Ones, [who] though in hiding still, shall join to our people once more and cause a new age to begin. End of Edict.

We also tell of the coming of Nebt Sekhmet Montu to the southern lands of Egypt at the time of the Star of Sirius arising . . .[1]

This legend is confirmed in the ancient traditions of the Dogons of Mali who are quite specific as to where their celestial visitors hailed from since they showed them a simple diagram of the complete Siriun system, just as the Ammonites describe, details of which have only become known to astronomers in recent years. A similar legend is also shared by the Bambara and Bozo tribes. On the other side of the Atlantic the Hopi Indians are positive in their assertion that their ancestors descended 'from the skies' having left their home in 'blue star Kachina', their name for Sirius, in order to bestow their blessings on Earth. There are many similar legends worldwide which may or may not have stemmed from the Atlantean original.

I found the Ammonite allusion to writing with fingers of fire, travelling in the air without wings and moving rivers out of their courses *by thought* of particular interest. Whoever these people were, they appear to have possessed powers of flight, a knowledge of sonics (Hekau) that could be applied either mechanically or *vocally*, and the ability to exercise the power of their own minds over material objects. Atlantean priests or Siriun space visitors? Either might fit the bill since the former were also skilled in sonics and mind power and had probably mastered aerial flight during the latter part of the Age of Leo. As for the latter, if the Sirius system was responsible for the seeding of this solar system either via panspermia or more direct contact, then it would seem logical to suppose that such beings might sustain a continued interest in the progress of their progeny. My readers must make up their own minds, but for my own part I incline towards a combination of the two. The Atlantean civilization might well have been founded by Siriuns, in which case it is not inconceivable that, foreseeing the oncoming disaster, beings from Sirius could have rescued some of their more promising specimens and deposited them safely in Egypt or wherever, to ensure the continuation of their genetic line. After all, as any zoologist will tell you, this would appear to be the prime aim of most animals and we are, after all, simply another branch of the species *mammalia*.

Regarding the Atlantean leonine divinity Khiet-Sîn (Sekhmet), legend has it that she always puts in an appearance when some great catastrophe is approaching, or our planet is due for an evolutionary quantum leap. She is certainly making her energies felt these days, but this is only to be expected, since she is the archetypal Essence of the Lion People of Sirius who have been allotted the task of coming to the aid of Gaia (Danuih) since their sister star, our Sun, first gave birth to her planetary brood all those eons ago (and let's face it, Gaia [Danuih] certainly needs her help today!). The Atlantean priests, of course, being in such close touch with Danuih, were well aware of how her and her parent's energies were being misused, and the pain this was causing their planetary genius and her stellar parent. They also knew how to invoke Khiet-Sîn. When we are threatened, we often use any means at our disposal to rid ourselves of our attackers, and it would seem logical to assume that Danuih might well react in a similar way, which in itself constitutes a warning note!

Endnote
1. Hope, M. *Ancient Egypt: The Sirius Connection*, p.59.

11. ATLANTIS: ITS ULTIMATE FATE

What *did* cause the final sinking of Atlantis? Numerous theories have been offered by scholars, researchers and psychics over the centuries, some of which are decidedly 'way out' and hardly in keeping with established scientific facts concerning the early growth and development of our planet. On the other hand some highly feasible suggestions have been offered, some of which can be accounted for empirically, so the fairest thing to do would be to outline the information to hand so that the reader may effect his or her own judgement in the matter.

Asteroids, Comets and other Extraterrestrial Intruders
Atlantologists who have sought proof of their theories within the discipline of science appear to have narrowed their choice down to two possibilities. The first of these, much favoured by the Viennese scientist and rocket expert Dr Otto Muck, and supported by several Russian authorities, is that the Earth was struck by a giant asteroid with such force that its axial rotation was affected. Muck backs his arguments with some sound scientific facts coupled with logical deduction, and brings geological and oceanographical evidence to bear in support of his theories. Other scholars and scientists who veer towards Muck's explanation include Colonel Braghine, Wyston, and Count Carlo de Lalande, and in more recent times Professor Vetchinkin of the Soviet Union. In his book *The Secret of Atlantis* Muck supplies the kind of facts and figures that are in keeping with a scientist of his discipline,

who worked as a member of the Peenemunde Rocket Research Team in Germany during World War II. Legend and mythology also add support to Muck's claims. Other researchers have tended to favour the intrusion of a giant meteorite or planetesimal as the cause of the Atlantis disaster, and equally plausible arguments have been offered to fortify their arguments.

Axis Tilts

The axis tilt theory is supported by Hapgood and Warlow among others, and certainly makes sense, although it could be seen to combine with both Hoerbiger's Lunar theory and Muck's asteroid in that some external intrusion was responsible for the tilt. On the other hand, there is the teaching of the ancient Greek sages, who believed that the Earth changes the angle of its axis every ten thousand years or thereabouts in the natural process of its evolution. This would accord with James Lovelock's Gaia hypothesis on the one hand, and Plato's inference that the regular increase and decrease of the human race is no coincidence, some governing intelligence taking a hand in the balancing operation on the other. As we have discussed in earlier chapters, the axis tilt theory is well supported in myth and legend, while evidence from ancient calendars and other fragments of scientific information that have filtered through via archaeological and geological sources also comes down on this side.

Chaos Science

According to chaos science, quantum evolutionary mishaps are likely to occur from time to time, such aberrations involving all life forms within a wide radius. One such cosmic hiccup might well have occurred at the time of the sinking of Atlantis. Likewise the genetic mutations commented upon by some psychics, that are supposed to have taken place in latter-day Atlantis, might also have resulted from some quantum calamity rather than base experimentation by errant scientists of the period.

Lunar Theories

Although Professor Hans Hoerbiger, whose theories were popular in the 1920s and 1930s, pioneered the idea that it was the capture of our Moon that caused the axis tilt that resulted in the sinking of Atlantis, according to Colonel Braghine the ancient Greeks were well acquainted with his theory concerning a Preselenite Age. Hoerbiger's ideas were strongly supported by H.S. Bellamy, and in more recent times by the French scholar Professor Denis Saurat. (See also Chapter 5).

Myth and Legend

It would take a complete book to do justice to the evidence from myth and folklore that supports both the Mu-an and Atlantean legends and their subsequent catastrophes. Some of these I have covered in earlier chapters although a more comprehensive list is to be found in *Atlantis: Myth or Reality* which concentrates on empirical evidence and avoids the more metaphysical aspects of the study. For the detailed researcher, works referenced in the Bibliographies of both books will serve to fill in any gaps.

One particularly interesting piece of information from the writings of Diodorus Siculus, deserves mention. According to Diodorus, on the death of Uranus, Basilea, the sister of Atlas, was unanimously elected Queen of Atlantis. Spence continues the tale:

> She espoused her brother Hyperion – that is, Lucifer – and bore him Helio and Selene, later the gods of the sun and moon. But her remaining brothers, dreading that Hyperion, her husband, might usurp the throne, slew him and drowned the infant Helio. Selene, in despair at the death of her brother, cast herself down from a height and perished. [1]

Are we being told that the solar-orientated religion of Atlantis was dashed beneath the waves, and that some kind of disaster overtook the moon at the same time? It bears thinking about.

Metaphysical Sources

Assuming that there was such a place as Atlantis, and that it disappeared in some earth-shattering catastrophe, was the cause purely 'material' or were there more metaphysical connotations involved? Well, it really depends on whether one separates spirit from matter. I do not. Physical occurrences are simply manifestations of spiritual designations – as above, so below – a major catastrophe signifying some imbalances at the subtle levels. Plato indicated that the Atlanteans had in some way offended the Deity, while the Biblical version of the Flood, like the Sumerian texts from which it was borrowed, also suggest that prior to the event mankind was misbehaving in some way that was offensive to the Creator; certain cosmic laws were being broken which had the effect of releasing the negative or chaotic energies of mass destruction. In his book *Memories and Visions of Paradise*, Richard Heinberg writes:

> . . . nearly every tradition ascribes the loss of Paradise to the appearance of some tragic aberration in the attitude or behaviour of human beings. While in the Golden Age they had been 'truth-speaking' and 'self-subdued,' living 'with no evil desires, without guilt or crime,' they now succumbed to suspicion, fear, greed, mistrust, and violence.
> But how did this change of character come about? Though purporting to describe a historical event, the ancients' descriptions of the cause of the Fall were nearly always cast in metaphors and allegories. As noted earlier, among these stories the most frequently encountered themes are disobedience, the eating of forbidden fruit, and forgetting (spiritual amnesia). [2]

In other words, mankind is its own worst enemy.

Genetic Reasons?
Plato saw the above-mentioned aberration in genetic terms:

> By such reflections, and by the continuance in them of the divine nature, all that we have described waxed and increased in them; but when this divine portion began to fade away in them, and became diluted too often, and with too much of the mortal admixture, and the human nature got the upper hand, then, they being unable to bear their fortune came unseemly, and to him who had an eye to see, they began to appear base, and had lost the fairest of their precious gifts; but to those who had no eye to see the true happiness, they still appeared glorious and blessed at the very time when they were filled with unrighteous avarice and power . . . [3]

Spence suggests that this interbreeding took place between the Atlanteans themselves, members of the upper caste foregoing their former exclusivity and mating with the lower caste aboriginals. This does not make sense, however, since the various castes had managed to live together harmoniously for several thousand years prior to the latter days. The explanation given by Plato, on the one hand, and Helio Arcanophus on the other, sounds far more feasible.

Channelled, and Other Extra-Sensory and PSI Accounts
Let us now examine some of the information that has issued from various psychic sources, starting with Helio Arcanophus'

comments, as channelled by British sensitive Tony Neate.

Tony Neate

Any nation or community that becomes too extreme will meet its end uncomfortably. The early Atlanteans became so spiritual, so philosophically minded that by the time trouble came to their shores they had no idea how to cope with it and were overwhelmed by the lesser-evolved infiltrators with their dubious intentions. Those who undergo work of an occult or psychic nature undergo a series of initiatory experiences by which they learn to combat negative forces and protect themselves against undesirable influences. In such a way they become immune to certain mental attacks, just as in modern medical practice the physical body is immunised against disease by building a resistance to it. This of course applies on every level for if lessons are not learned in life and people are too sheltered they become vulnerable to attack of any kind as they have no recognition of the enemy and therefore no defensive measures. Atlantis in the latter days was a perfect example of these practical deficiencies.

It is no use having an ideal if one is not prepared to see that it is honoured, for sooner or later both the idealist and the ideal will fall before the thoughts and ideals of others who are less sympathetic. Yet humanity today has gone to the other extreme; the material world has become his god. Highly dangerous weapons of attack and defence are made and used and beliefs are forced on others. Human beings need to aim for a balance in all things, and particularly for balance between the material and spiritual aspects of all sides of life . . .

Immigrants came to Atlantis from lesser evolved lands and started to take an interest in the strange powers possessed by this handsome race. But those early Atlanteans were not prepared for such an influx and, because of their great trust they allowed many people to come to their country so long as they abided by the rules of the State and were not belligerent. As the years went by many of these lesser evolved people from other lands intermarried with the evolved Atlanteans. The story of the 'sons of god and the daughters of men' recorded in the Bible actually originated in these happenings.

As the evolutionary level fell the lesser evolved began to learn the occult secrets that had assisted Atlantis towards the path of greatness, but they had neither the wisdom nor the spiritual maturity to control the forces they were tampering with . . .

'The gap widened; on one side the high priest and his followers pursued the paths of truth and righteousness and, on the other, in the backwoods and secret places, the renegade priests practised, perpetuating foul ceremonies through which they could obtain power over the ordinary people. The true priests tried hard to fight back, but, as is often the case when the evolved come up against the unevolved, it is the latter who appear to win as the former are limited to spiritually pure methods of defence. With black magic spread degeneracy and debauchery. The ordinary people became afraid of these priests of the Left Hand Path, afraid of what they would do to them if they did not obey their commands . . .[4]

Helio Arcanophus then went on to explain how certain signs and portents in the sky alerted the wise priests of the forthcoming catastrophe. Seismic disturbance of a magnitude hitherto unknown started to rack the continent, while perturbations had been observed in the regular orbit of a certain celestial body that boded ill to the Atlantean astronomers. Although little heed was paid to all this by the general populace, the believers set about making arrangements to flee to lands which their psychic sources had indicated to be safe. Atlantis already had thriving colonies in Egypt, South America, Spain and many areas of the Mediterranean, and it was to these distant shores that many Atlanteans made their way, as directed by the Priests of Light. According to Helio Arcanophus, the celestial body in question was destined to become the Moon we now know today, and it was this body's movement to a closer proximity to Earth that caused the axis tilt and the acquisition of the five extra days.

George Ch. Pisanis

A recent publication from The Spiritualist Society of Athens features a series of communications received through the Greek medium George Ch. Pisanis during the 1960s, in which he claims to have been overshadowed by the spirits of Archimedes, and Solon of Athens, with comments by Thales of Miletus. According to these sources Atlantis was governed by women (The Cancerian Age?), while much emphasis is placed on the advanced science of the Old Country, which is described as being way ahead of anything we have today. These phenomenal developments in science and technology are seen as prime contributors to the final destruction and Fall of the island continent because, while all these amazing experiments were taking place:

. . . the depravity both moral and spiritual had reached its acme. Compassion, love and affection no longer existed, and their place was taken by lust, degeneracy and prostitution. Atlantis was on the edge of the abyss. We few could do nothing to prevent this corruption. Together with the initiates we planned from which part of the country they should make their exit to new uninhabited territories, in order to save part at least of their civilization when this had reached its final stage. Fortunately, dear readers, when what we foresaw actually took place, I no longer existed: I had been recalled to heaven . . .

As you know, in the time of the venerable Solon Atlantis was at the height of its glory. From then on, after the death of Solon and when many years had passed, the development and the vast progress made by the scientists gradually undermined the initial Laws of justice, and although Atlantis made huge strides in its technological achievements, its decline dated from that time. [5]

The entity then goes on to describe the corruptive influences that accompanied the development of scientific expertise and leaves us with the following thought:

Everyone today is of the opinion that Egypt was the enlightener in its time of the world of the spirit. But it was not the Egyptians; it was the priests of Atlantis, the Initiates, who escaped in time to the four corners of the World. A number of them belong to the Greek People, for they were the first inhabitants of your country and came into it from three sides. Also, the language of Atlantis possessed the letters of the Greek alphabet – not as many as there are today but many more. And many words in their language are references to ancient lost books of the Chaldeans and other races . . .

Do not seek for Atlantis in the Mediterranean, but in the Sahara and in the Atlantic Ocean, where a large section of it sank to vast depths . . . [6]

Edgar Cayce

It has been observed that many of the life readings given by Cayce deal specifically with the latter-day period of Atlantis, probably because Cayce himself was in incarnation there at the time as were many of those closely associated with him. This is to be expected, however, since members of group souls tend to incarnate together. Cayce's alter ego speaks of the land breaking up in three stages, which accords with Lewis Spence's theory, and gives the date of approximately 10000 BC for the second stage. Also mentioned are the movements of numbers of people to lands that were deemed to be safe; Egypt, Portugal, France and Spain receiving the first waves of Atlantean immigrants, and the Americas providing safe haven for later colonies of survivors. Yucatan and parts of Arizona are also mentioned. Aside from comments regarding the misuse of solar and crystal energy, and the fact that the Atlantean land mass was suffering severe seismic disturbances, Cayce does not appear to refer to the intervention of an extraterrestrial body although, as we have previously observed, he does state that the axis of the Earth was at a very different angle from what it is today as a result of which Atlantis lay in the southern hemisphere.

The Theosophical Society – Helena Blavatsky

Theosophy designates our present race as the Fifth, or Aryan Race, the Fourth Race being the great race of Atlantis. Catastrophes such as those experienced by Mu and Atlantis have not as yet appeared on Fifth Race horizons, although my own opinion, which is shared with many others in this day and age, is that we may shortly be bidding a fond farewell to the period of comparative stability we have enjoyed since the Old Country last showed its face to the Sun. According to the Theosophists, the destruction of Atlantis was caused by a series of catastrophes, the final one of which occurred around 9464 BC. The task of putting together the channelled details on both Atlantis and Mu or Lemuria, fell to Colonel W. Scott-Elliott, whose book *The Story of Atlantis* was first published in Benares, India, in 1890. Copies of this book are still available through specialized outlets such as Magis Books in Loughborough and The Atlantis Bookshop in London, and the four maps supplied with it are certainly worth studying. Recent research in the areas of the North Sea and the Atlantic seabed, coupled with Hapgood's study of the movement of the Poles and the old Sea Maps have, however, served to bring the Atlantean event much nearer to our present times than the dates offered by the Theosophists. For example, Scott-Elliott quotes the first great Atlantean catastrophe as having occurred some 800,000 years ago; the second around 200,000 years ago and the third and final as mentioned by Plato – 80,000 years ago. The work of Churchward, Braghine, Muck and others also refutes these extremely ancient datings.

The Theosophical material on Atlantis is lengthy and detailed, and a little too Mu-an (the Indian influence, no doubt) for my consumption. Not that this is a bad thing in itself, but since Mu and Atlantis were such vastly different cultures I do feel that a clear distinction should be effected. Where the Theosophical story does slot into place with most other inspired information on the subject is in their belief in the large-scale degeneration that took place in the latter days, the energies generated from which were seen to contribute to the final break-up of the Atlantean lands.

Anthroposophy – Rudolf Steiner

Steiner seems to have shared many of the views expressed by the Theosophists prior to setting up his own organization. In his book *Cosmic Memory* he devotes a chapter to what he refers to as 'our Atlantean ancestors' who, he assures us, differed considerably from present-day people. Steiner falls into that category of mystics who conceived of the Atlanteans as being predominantly right-brain orientated, left-brain logic and reason being totally absent in their psychological economy. By way of compensation, he sees them as having been imbued with exceptional powers of memory!

Steiner claims to have gained his information concerning the early days of the Earth from the Akashic Records, which he incorporated in a series of essays entitled *From the Akasha Chronicle*. This question of Akasha is ever a thorny one for the sceptic and there are times when the whole concept bothers me – unless it can be taken in the more scientific context of the existence of bands of timelessness (seen by some as Black Holes in which time as we know it is suspended).

With so many people claiming access to what is viewed by many psychics and mystics as an infinite fount of universal knowledge, and producing totally contradictory results, one cannot dismiss the psychological angles. Wishful thinking and a vivid imagination sparked off, perhaps, by some products of Hollywood celluloid, must surely have contributed much to this kind of viewing. Witness the number of make-believe characters from the world of cinema and television that have surfaced via certain channellers of late, each claiming access to 'Akasha'! The truth most probably lies in the fact that we may only access that to which our genetic memory banks, or experiences in other time-zones, provides us with the necessary codes. After all, a computer is only as good as its program, and our brains are really nothing more than complex computers built into our physical bodies for the purpose of pushing the appropriate buttons and pulling the right strings. If that computer 'loops', we may suffer physical or mental breakdowns until its silicon chips (brain cells) are either repaired or reprogrammed. And as everyone knows, a computer has to be programmed by some external mind or intelligence, which leads us full circle to the psyche or spirit and *its* stage of spiritual maturity. So, no matter how clever we may be (how many terminals our brain-computers may display), unless we have the wisdom (soul-age) to effect the use of those additional facilities (to access right-brain knowledge), we will find our intelligence sadly limited to the left-brain logic of the material world. Journeys to the Akasha during altered states of consciousness are therefore more likely to present the viewer with what he or she wants to see rather than what is or was.

Steiner concurs with the Theosophical teachings regarding the various root races and their subdivisions, and the ultimate fate of Atlantis. His doctrines do carry a distinctly Christian bias, however, which tends to confirm my views expressed in the preceding paragraphs.

Daphne Vigers

Miss Vigers' book *Atlantis Rising* was first published in 1944 when the author was in her mid-twenties. To my knowledge she has never written anything since. More's the pity, as her inspired writing carries a quality seldom encountered in modern mystics; a combination of sincerity, wonder and simplicity that seems to elude many an aspiring guru. However, a guru was exactly what Miss Vigers did *not* want to be, so following the publication of her book she promptly retreated into obscurity. Her guiding entity went by the name of Helio-Arkhan, which name bears a close resemblance to Tony Neate's contact, although I can assure my readers that at the time H.A. (as he is affectionately called) effected his initial contact with us neither Tony, nor any of the other founder members of The Atlantean had ever heard of Daphne Vigers and her book (which says something for the quality of both channellings). Vigers' account of Atlantis is also very similar to that channelled through Tony, and her description of the Latter Days is both poignant and incisive.

Vigers falls into that category of psychics who associate the buried Atlantean energies with a specific ethos, in this case that of Britain, which is hardly surprising since our country was engaged in a World War at the time and the national spirit was therefore very much to the fore. However, while it is all very cosy to conceive of Britain as being the birthplace of the New Atlantis, it should also be borne in mind that we are not alone in this claim. Many Americans assure me that their great land is the chosen place for the rise of the new Atlantean Ray, while I have also met and talked with mystics from Spain, France, Scandinavia and North Africa who are convinced that the Atlantean time-capsule that is destined shortly to be opened was buried upon their hallowed shores. We shall just have to wait and see, shall we not!

Phyllis Cradock
The channelling that resulted in Ms Cradock's (Fanny Cradock of 1950s and 1960s TV fame) Atlantean novels *Gateway to Remembrance*, *The Eternal Echo* and *The Immortal Hour* took place some time prior to her period in the public eye with her husband, Johnny. These three books deal mainly with the Latter Days of Atlantis, and are certainly worth perusing if one is to reach an unbiased conclusion regarding information from extra-sensory sources.

Brad Steiger
The American writer, Brad Steiger, is perhaps better known for his ideas concerning the intrusion of extraterrestrials into earthly affairs. His book *Atlantis Rising* explores the various facets of the Atlantean legend, in which he sees E.T.s as having played an important role. His conjectures are based on his own intuition, plus channellings on the subject received through Francie Steiger and the well known American medium Joseph Donnelly and his associates. The aspects covered include the Atlantean language, why Atlantis sank, the true symbolism of the pyramid (which was apparently completely misunderstood by the ancient Egyptians), other sunken lands including Mu/Lemuria and two at the North and South Poles, axis tilts and so forth, a distinction being effected between those cataclysms that are brought about by natural sources and those that were purely mankind's doing – according to Donnelly's psychic contacts, that is!

Frank Alper
'Dr' Frank Alper is one of a crop of popular American channellers who attract large followings. His psychic contact goes by the name of 'Adamis' who, according to the back cover of Alper's book, has appointed himself '. . .the spiritual name of "Christos", which means "The Enlightened One"'. (I always understood the word Christos to mean 'anointed'!) Alper has published three books on the subject of Atlantis, and I have to confess that after perusing Volume 1, I found myself at such variance with his teachings, especially concerning animals and other life forms, that I saw little use in pursuing the study further, and am therefore not competent to comment on Volumes 2 and 3.

I suppose it all depends on whether one prefers the more logical approach that is backed by some degree of empirical evidence, or whether one is prepared to go 'over the top' and accept anything that might issue from supposed 'higher' intelligences. Surely a balanced approach is the best in the long run, since many of the views, 'memories', and other psi orientated impressions mentioned in this book, including my own, might well be proven incorrect in the fullness of time. Human consciousness being not, as yet anyway, a perfect machine, good intentions and sincerity alone do not guarantee truth. A small child describing an historical pageant might relate his experience in terms unrecognizable to adults and yet to him they would be as valid as his perception and the development of his powers of comparison would allow. And so it is with soul-age. I am also of the opinion that much of what passes as recollections of past experiences in legendary civilizations on Earth relates to either parallel existences in unseen universes or lives in some other part of the visible universe.

Many other well known and highly respected psychics and occultists have commented on what they believe to have been their former Atlantean lives, notably Dion Fortune and Christine Hartley, while Tarot specialist Gareth Knight made a tape recording for public consumption which deals with information which he claims to have obtained from the former. Since I have commented on these 'revelations' in some depth in *Atlantis – Myth or Reality*, I feel it would be unfair to effect a repeat, but anyone interested could, I am sure, obtain a copy of the tape in question from Gareth Knight.

There are, of course, many other organizations that feature the Atlantis legend in their teachings or esoterica, The Rosicrucians and The Golden Triangle Fellowship being two examples that spring to mind. Esoteric teachers of the calibre of Mary Long and Dr Mona Rolfe have also covered Atlantiana in their books, so there is no shortage of material for the serious student to sort through. Many impressions of the Old Country have obviously percolated through down the ages from the collective unconscious, and if I have neglected to comment on someone's particular favourite it should be seen in the context of space being at a premium rather than taken as a judgement.

Personal Experiences

The question of my own subjective experiences during altered states of consciousness, dreams and so forth is bound to arise, and although I am reluctant to include these I am aware that this will be expected of me. However, I will endeavour to keep them to a minimum. Yes, I do recall Atlantis, if indeed it was the Atlantis of this planet and I am inclined to think that it might have been. My Atlantis shared much in common with the place described by Daphne Vigers in her book *Atlantis Rising*, and with the land of Tony Neate's Helio Arcanophus, which is understandable, I suppose, since 'H.A.' has been one of my most important Teachers since childhood and it was to him that the dedication of *Atlantis – Myth or Reality* refers. The name 'Helio Arcanophus', incidentally, is titular, and simply means 'Chief High Priest of Helio' or Ruler of Atlantis.

There were certainly no slaves, gross experiments in genetic engineering, atomic power stations or anything of that kind around, and the priesthood functioned much along the lines I have described in Chapter 10. People were mainly fair-haired and blue-eyed although there were some copper-skinned, green-eyed tribes in the northwest, while the peoples of the eastern coastline were often dark-haired and violet-eyed. Consequently, one could encounter a mixture of these colourings. Atlantean faces had a Mongolian type of appearance in that they featured high cheekbones and slanted eyes which, when accompanied by long, thick blond hair and blue eyes gave a somewhat unusual appearance. People were also very tall, the average height for an adult male being seven feet or more, and obesity was seldom, if ever, encountered. My recollections of the capital accord with Plato's description, and the same goes for the circular buildings, canals and waterways, and blue/white/gold/robes of the priesthood.

A moon or moonlight I do not recall, but the rays of the daytime sunshine were much more silvery than gold, giving daylight a much 'lighter' appearance. I was part of a close family unit that has spiritual origins in some place other than Earth (which I *do* recall), and my visit to the Atlantean island continent was my first time here. I am therefore not qualified to comment on any episode in earlier or later Mu-an or Atlantean history. Nor have I ever made a point of probing the 'Akasha' in search of such information, my energies having being employed in the pursuit of my karma. Besides, enough psychics seem to have engaged in this somewhat suspect exercise, so why add to the confusion! I do recall a vague memory stirring the first time I ever heard Atlantis mentioned, and when I subsequently came across a book describing the latter days I cried bitterly: it was like suddenly reading that some beautiful city one had left in one's childhood had been cruelly desecrated and totally obliterated. But I was not there to witness these events as they read as new and strange to me. More easily I recall the latter days of my old and much loved planet – in the natural course of its evolution – but that is another story.

Endnotes

1. Spence, L. *The Occult Sciences in Atlantis*, pp.18–19.
2. Heinberg, R. *Memories and Visions of Paradise*, p.89.
3. Donnelly, I. *Atlantis: The Antediluvian World*, pp.19–20.
4. *Atlantis: Past and to Come*, channelled by Tony Neate, pp.29–31.
5. Pisanis, G.C. (trs. John Alexander). *The Lost Civilization of Atlantis*, pp.92–3.
6. Ibid. pp.93–4.

12. WILL ATLANTIS RISE AGAIN?

Prophecies relating to the end of the world have been with us since time immemorial, each generation embroidering its own forewarnings of impending doom on the tapestry of Time. These warnings of some inevitable catastrophe have appeared with such regularity that they are now dismissed as the ravings of the lunatic fringe, and as such provide the popular press with a fair target for scornful amusement, or derision. Although the 'end of the world theme' is well and truly spelled out in the Bible, most Christians, when questioned regarding such predictions, usually dismiss them as relating to some age centuries hence when our Star eventually burns out and its planetary children depart with it. However, all disaster forecasts do not relate to the end of our planet as such, but rather to violent and drastic changes that are likely to affect its surface and, therefore, the lives of those that dwell thereon. The hell-fire and 'wrath of God' warnings of Fundamentalism have found their equivalent in recent years in the nuclear doom prognostications of the peace marchers and the eco-orientated protests of those who are willing to lend an ear to the implications of the impending Greenhouse Effect.

From the Atlantean and Mu-an disasters, however, we may observe that even major cataclysmic upheavals have their survivors, who are subsequently required to adjust to the new conditions that inevitably follow in the wake of something of the magnitude of an axis tilt. Should Gaia choose to stir in her orbital resting place, this does not necessarily imply that life as we know it will cease to exist, although it could mean that certain species which have become an irritant to her body, and as such an impediment to her own evolutionary plan, might well be ejected in the process, as may be evidenced in the extinction of the dinosaurs. The trouble is that mankind has followed the Biblical Lucifer in seeing itself alone as created in the image of its Maker and, therefore, aspired to a kind of false spiritual supremacy that has served to isolate it from the rest of creation, including the very entity that gives it life and nourishment. Coming events inevitably cast their shadows, and since our right brains have an inbuilt propensity for accessing Timelessness, there is bound to be some unconscious prompting therefrom that alerts us to the imminence of forthcoming disaster, that is, if we are sufficiently sensitive to its message. We may couch this awareness in sociological, religious, ethnic, or metaphysical terms as befits our environmental conditioning, but deep down in the collective unconscious of mankind is the sure knowledge that Chaos inevitably precedes Order and vice versa, and that sooner or later old ways are bound to give way to new ones, in both the microcosmic/personal, or macrocosmic/universal context.

The 'Atlantis Rising' theme has grown apace over the last fifty years, which is hardly surprising since we are now well on target for the bulls-eye of Chaos. There have been a number of books, not all of which have issued from the pens of the metaphysically inclined, that either feature the idea as a title or foster it within their pages. For example, many science fiction writers utilize their craft as a vehicle for the expression of those beliefs that might in the ordinary course of life condemn them to the lunatic fringe. Likewise, scientists and clerics have confided in me their belief in Atlantis of the past, and the future, on the strict understanding that I respect their confidence. Atlantis is so deeply embedded in the human psyche that try as we may to rationalize it away it has the habit of reappearing in each age under different guises.

The Edgar Cayce Prophecies
Edgar Cayce's alter ego had no compunction about foretelling the eventual rise of Atlantis from its watery bed, and that this would occur during major upheavals effecting severe physical changes. These will include:

- The breaking up of the Earth on the western side of America.
- The sinking into the sea of the greater portion of Japan.

- Upheavals in the Arctic and Antarctic leading to a shifting of the poles which will result in frigid and semi-tropical areas becoming more tropical.
- The reappearance of lands in both the Pacific and Atlantic Oceans.
- Many of the battlefields of World War II will be turned to ocean with seas, islands, bays, etc.
- The disappearance of whole portions of the east coast of New York, with New York city itself all but disappearing.
- Southern portions of Carolina and Georgia will also vanish.
- The waters of the Great Lakes will empty into the Gulf of Mexico.
- The Earth will be broken up in many places, the physical aspects of the West coast of America being particularly affected. Dry land will appear in the Caribbean Sea. South America will be shaken badly from top to bottom. [1]

For those interested, fuller details of these changes are to be found in the book *Edgar Cayce on Atlantis* (see Bibliography).

Daphne Vigers' Vision

In her book *Atlantis Rising* Daphne Vigers gives a moving but terrifying account of the rebirth of the Old Country which she witnessed in the company of her Guide and Mentor, the Atlantean High priest Helio Arkhan:

Now I went forward in time and watched Atlantis rise from her watery tomb.

Great storms raged and the earth quaked in parts that had never before experienced convulsions within the memory of this age. So widespread was the disturbance that many thought that the earth had begun to disintegrate and that the end of its life-span had been reached. I went to the place where Atlantis was, and as I looked upon the roaring waters three giant water-spouts hurled themselves to the heavens from the south, south-east and north of the Atlantic. Huge whirlpools formed, throwing cascades of fish and sea-creatures upon the surface of the waters.

For miles the sea was like an ocean of frothy milk, then slowly and majestically the rocks of the Atlantean coast-line emerged. Thick mud, silvered with the bodies of fishes, streamed off the edges.

Again the waters thundered, tossing angry spray miles into the air, as though reluctant to give up their prize.

The swirl and roar of the ocean echoed for miles and could be heard in other continents.

The terror and magnificence of this gigantic resurrection reminded me of my feelings whilst watching the last hours of Atlantis centuries before.

Three great sharks lay expiring on the newly risen land. I saw strange and grotesque monsters of the deep lying on the wet mud that covered the bosom of Atlantis.

Forests of seaweed piled up in tangled masses on the jutting points of the rocks, moving with the wriggling shoals of fish they had enmeshed. Up rose the volcano that I had watched before do mighty battle with the sea, its surface smothered with barnacles, slime, and black seaweed, and on a ridge a long-wrecked ship lay balanced. Gradually the slime of mud, seaweeds, sea-anemones and the chaos of dead marine life was swept off the coastal ridges by the still angry waters. But now it seemed they knew they were fighting a losing battle, for more and more of Atlantis had risen out of the clutch of their grasping liquid hands.

On a mud waste a whale was flailing its giant body in its vain efforts to reach the sea again. The sight was horrible to watch.

As more of the continent emerged I thought I saw the still-standing pillars of an Atlantean temple. At the top of a mound of seaweed-adorned mud, a peak of pyramid showed, the white stone brilliant in the sunlight. Now I was able to discern the rise and fall of the land. Coral encrusted mountains reared up, valleys dipped gently down to the rivers, which, impeded by the mud and debris of fish carcasses, were moving but slowly.

Already the plains and highlands were drying. In the midst of a wilderness of mud a petrified tree stood in stark solitude.

Suddenly a bird, migrating from another land, perched on the top of the petrified trunk, resting on its journey. Soon a swarm of gulls hovered over the risen continent, and after circling for some time the leader gracefully swooped down and began scavenging the vast feast set before him; quickly the others followed.

Atlantis was having her grave-shroud pecked off her reborn body.

The waters quietened and diverted themselves into currents round the island continent. The sun was shining once again upon Atlantis and life dwelt upon her.[2]

When I first read this account many years ago I was deeply moved. It was rather like hearing that a loved one who had been given up for dead had suddenly been found alive, and there was joy in my heart. But I also realized that the process of this rebirth of Atlantis would also bring about the demise of millions, and create great suffering for the immediate survivors. Vigers writes of the new race of Atlanteans which will succeed its Aryan predecessors, and which could probably be equated with the Theosophists' sixth root race. These will be the people destined to inherit the post-tilt world, those spirits whose soul-ages designate them the rightful heirs to the bosom of Gaia herself, who will live in peaceful co-existence with her, treat her wounds with loving care, and harvest her bounty for the ensuing, physically and spiritually rich Age of Order.

Helio Arcanophus through Tony Neate (channelled in 1957)

Atlantis will rise again, be it the physical land itself or the spiritual essence of those former days. Ask yourself truthfully whether you belong to the selfish materialism of today or to the new world of the future that will be built on tolerance and brotherly love, an existence free from belligerence in which harmony and beauty reign supreme and the minds of men are not distorted and narrowed by greed. If you feel you are part of such a future then start working for it now. The Atlanteans of the past achieved it. Do not let it slip from your hands as it did from theirs. [3]

Ancient Greek Sources

According to the Greek historians, cataclysmic ends to great civilizations occur every 10,000 years. Plato mentions how the gods purge the Earth from time to time, the elements of fire and water featuring particularly in these cleansing sessions. If we take into account some of the dates estimated for the final Atlantean inundation, Dr Muck's 8489 BC for example, or even the later dates proposed by Spence, Mooney, Ivimy and others, it would seem that we are uncomfortably close to the extreme arc of the pendulum's swing to Chaos.

The Berbers

The Berbers have an ancient tradition which tells how their homeland, which originally lay off the coast of Africa, sank beneath the waves, where it will not remain forever, since fate has decreed that it shall rise at some unspecified time in the future.

The Amerindians

Several Amerindian tribes, notably the Hopi, share the belief that the island in the ocean to the east, from which their ancestors originally came, is destined to see daylight once again, the time for its uprising being almost upon us.

Nostradamus, Mother Shipton, and the Prophecy of The Fox
Better known among the 'prophets of doom' are Nostradamus and
Mother Shipton, both of whom appear to have committed
themselves to a date somewhere around the end of the present
millennium. One of the problems with seers of this kind, however,
is that they have tended to mask their knowledge of the future in
obscure couplets or quatrains which only appear obvious after the
event. I am also inclined to think that in some cases the necessity
to effect a good rhyme can take the place of accuracy although as
any time-traveller knows, trying to pinpoint events witnessed in
the unrelated dimensions of Outer Time on an earthly calendar is
almost impossible, exact dates only proving correct by sheer fluke.
This should not be blamed on some flaw in the psychic talent of
the seer, but rather on those ring-pass-nots that inevitably govern
major evolutionary cycles.

The Fox's Prophecy, sometimes ascribed to an ancient Briton
by the name of Haro, is lesser known. It is believed to cover a
period of some 5,000 years and is exclusive to Britain and the
British ethos. It is produced in full in Robert Scrutton's book
Secrets of Lost Atland pages 147-150, but germane to our present
enquiry are the final five verses:

Taught wisdom by disasters,
England shall learn to know
That trade is not the only gain
Heaven gives to man below.

The greed for gold departed,
The golden calf cast down,
Old England's sons again shall rise
The altar and the crown.

Rejoicing seas shall welcome
Their mistress once again;
Again the banner of St.George
Shall rule upon the main . . .

Again in hall and homestead
Shall joy and peace be seen
And smiling children raise again
The maypole on the green. [4]

Scrutton reads Frisian overtones into these final verses, the Cross of St George being identical to the old Mu-an/Atlantean Sun Cross, and the 'mistress' referred to being the Frisian Goddess Frya (Norse Freya?). Equally one could read 'Atlantean' into both contexts, Frya probably being synonymous with the Atlantean Heliona or Danuih. The Frisian lands were probably a colony of Atlantis, anyway, so it is 'the same difference', as the saying goes.

A New Race of Atlanteans?

It has already been suggested from several sources that, following some impending world catastrophe involving an axis tilt, a new race of more highly evolved people will bring about an era of peace, love and harmony worldwide. This would suggest a major evolutionary quantum leap in which those younger souls who would not be able to handle the faster frequencies that Gaia herself will be emitting after such an event, will leave Earth for other cosmic 'nurseries' in which they will feel more at home until such times as they, too, are ready to accept an equivalent spiritual quantum leap. According to certain metaphysical teachings the gap between soul-ages on this planet is too wide for Gaia's comfort. At one extreme we have the mature psyches fighting for a peaceful, caring society in which the life force in all things is acknowledged and respected, while at the other end, violent, aberrated and destructive energies are manifesting through those younger souls who are not yet ready for, and therefore confused by, the vast changes that are taking place around them both spiritually and materially. Between these two extremes is the vast mass of humanity, unsure of which way to jump, the lure of Chaos beckoning them from one side, and the security of Order from the other. One point that should be mentioned as regards the Chaos-Order complex is that although Order is preferable to Chaos in that it is more comfortable to live with, especially at the material level, extremes of Order can sometimes prove restrictive to the human spirit. It is for this reason that many mystical teachers have suggested a 'Middle Way', from which aspect we can enjoy the peace of Order, and observe the lessons of Chaos without venturing into its kingdoms.

One thing I think we can be sure of, however, is that the Earth as an entity is *not* going to suffer demise in the near, or even distant future. The world Order as we know it may well pass, since nothing lasts forever, and the survivors will be those species, *Homo sapiens* included, who are able to adapt to the new conditions, whatever these might be. Some comfort is surely to be found in the prophetic words of Plutarch:

> . . . there will become a fated and predestined time when the earth will be completely levelled, united and equal, there will be but one mode of life and but one form of government among mankind who will all speak one language and will live happily.[5]

Many people have approached me recently with the request to compose a simple rite in the Atlantean idiom to help Gaia in the great suffering she is sustaining at the hands of those of our kind who are systematically stripping her body of its mineral wealth, stealing her forests, and raping her person, and effect a unification with her, her planetary sisters, her parent Star and other stellar relatives involved in the spiritual and somatic evolutionary processes taking place in our present-day world. In spite of my Atlantean connections I am not at heart a ritualist, but I fully appreciate the need felt by many to express their feelings of love, sorrow and gratitude in some outward, devotional and positive way. After much meditation and many prayers for guidance, I have written the following, which constitutes a prayer to Gaia (the Atlantean Danuih) for forgiveness, an invocation to Khiet-Sîn to intervene and prevent further ills being inflicted on Gaia's body and spirit, and an invocation to the male or female aspects of our Star, the Sun, to heal its daughter and help her through the dark days that lie ahead.

This is a simple rite that requires no complicated magical preparations, and can be said quietly before retiring, or in some outdoor, sylvan, place where the brown earth of Gaia's skin lies firmly beneath one's feet, or the stones of her bones protrude boldly against the skyline. Safety during this rite rests with the intention of the supplicant; love, caring, and a genuine feeling for Gaia automatically invoking her protection. Since we are working in the Atlantean idiom I shall use her Atlantean name of Danuih.

RITE FOR THE HEALING AND PROTECTION OF DANUIH, THE EARTH MOTHER

Having chosen your place for the performance of this rite, kneel down, and place the palms of your hands firmly on the ground. If you are performing the rite indoors, a crystal, rock, or even a humble pebble will do to take the place of the ground. Feel the life force flowing *from you* into the ground rather than the reverse. Then lean forward and press your forehead against the ground, crystal, or whatever, this time addressing Danuih through the chakric centres in your heart and head:

GREAT MOTHER DANUIH, WHO HAS SO GENEROUSLY ALLOWED OUR SPECIES TO EXPERIENCE LIFE ON YOUR BODY, WHICH IS THIS PLANET WE CALL EARTH, PLEASE FORGIVE THOSE OF OUR KIND WHO HAVE HARMED YOU AND CAUSED YOU SO MUCH SUFFERING, AND HELP US TO HELP THEM TO SEE THE ERRORS OF THEIR WAYS. PLEASE ACCEPT THIS SMALL OFFERING OF LOVE THAT I NOW GIVE YOU.

Direct your personal energies into channels of love and healing, and allow them to flow freely into the Earth (stone, crystal, etc.). After a moment or two you will begin to feel the power being returned to you with interest. Allow this exchange of energies between Danuih and yourself to last few a minute or so, then kiss the ground, stone, crystal, etc.) and thank Danuih for acknowledging your sincerity. When you have completed this part of the rite, raise your head, look upwards and address Khiet-Sîn:

I INVOKE YOU, CELESTIAL LIONESS, GUARDIAN OF THE JUST AND PROTECTOR OF THOSE WHO SERVE THE LIGHT, AND HUMBLY REQUEST YOUR DIVINE INTERVENTION, NOT FOR MYSELF, BUT FOR YOUR COSMIC SISTER, DANUIH, WHO IS SUFFERING AT THE HANDS OF MY SPECIES. I ASK THAT YOU FREE HER FROM HER OPPRESSORS SO THAT SHE MAY PROGRESS IN ACCORDANCE WITH THE AGE OF HER BODY AND SPIRIT. IN RETURN I GIVE YOU MY LOVE, AN ACKNOWLEDGEMENT OF THE POWER AND NATURE OF YOUR ENERGIES, AND A PROMISE TO WORK BY YOUR SIDE TO THIS END AS YOU IN YOUR WISDOM MAY DEEM FIT.

Raise your hands and place your two wrists together in a cupping position. Imagine a stream of energy rising out of your hands in the form of an orange coloured flame. After a few seconds you will sense another flame descending from Khiet-Sîn – it will be a blue flame, representing the cold-heat of nuclear fusion. Allow the two colours to vibrate side by side until Khiet-Sîn's energies start to fade. She will know just how much of her Ray you can take. Then withdraw your own energies and seal their exit by bringing the palms of your hands together as in a gesture of prayer. What you are actually doing is offering yourself as a channel through which Khiet-Sîn's energies may flow to Danuih. Then place your hands once more palms down on the earth, crystal, etc. and say:

DEAREST DANUIH, I HAVE ASKED KHIET-SIN TO HELP YOU AND SHE HAS ALLOWED ME TO ACCESS THESE, HER ENERGIES, WHICH I IN TURN PASS TO YOU.

Feel the power of Khiet-Sîn's blue flame and your own orange flame blend together and pass into the body of Danuih. She will acknowledge your double offering in some way special to you.

The final invocation in this rite is to the solar deity, who may also be invoked singly, depending on whether one is god- or goddess-orientated. The next prayer is to the feminine aspect of the Sun, as I feel there is an over-emphasis of the masculine in today's world. Assume the position of raised arms and head back as given in the Rites to the Sun in Chapter 8.

BRIGHT MOTHER, WHOSE WARM, EMBRACING RAYS BRING LIFE TO DANUIH, AND ALL THAT DWELL ON THE PLANET THAT IS HER BODY, WE, HER CHILDREN, ASK THAT YOU HELP HER THROUGH HER TIMES OF TRIAL THAT LIE AHEAD. HELP US TO HEAL HER WOUNDS, AND GIVE HER THE ENERGIES SHE WILL NEED TO MAKE THE FORTHCOMING SPIRITUAL AND PHYSICAL TRANSITION, AND STAND BY HER IN HER HOUR OF NEED. AND PLEASE, BRIGHT HELIONA, CONVEY THE CONCERN AND LOVE OF US MORTALS, WHO ARE YOUR CHILDREN AS MUCH AS HERS, TO YOUR PARENT, THE BLUE STAR, AND HER CELESTIAL COMPANION, WITHOUT WHOSE CREATIVE ENERGIES WE WOULD NEVER HAVE BEEN GRANTED THE OPPORTUNITY TO EXPERIENCE IN THESE PARTICULAR WORLDS OF MATTER. WE ASK YOUR WARMTH, YOUR LOVE, AND YOUR BLESSING FOR ALL WHO ARE ENTRUSTED IN YOUR CARE.

Pause for a moment to meditate and receive Heliona's acknowledgement of your petition, then slowly lower your arms and cross them over your chest as though you were holding the Pharoanic Crook and Flail depicted in Egyptian paintings. Slowly bow your head, and close the Rite as instructed in the *Dance to The Rising Sun* in Chapter 8, but substituting the Atlantean name Heliona (or Helio) for 'Star' in the closing 'Thanksgiving'.

FINI

Endnotes
1. Cayce, Edgar. *Edgar Cayce On Atlantis*, pp.159–60.
2. Vigers, D. *Atlantis Rising*, pp.144–5.
3. Stephen Taylor (ed.). *Atlantis, Past and To Come*.
4. Scrutton, R. *The Secrets of Lost Atland*, pp.149–50.
5. Tomas, A. *Atlantis – From Legend to Discovery*, p.133.

BIBLIOGRAPHY

Alper, Frank. *Exploring Atlantis*, Arizona Metaphysical Society, Phoenix, AZ, 1981.

Bellamy, H.S. *The Atlantis Myth*, Faber & Faber, London, 1948.

Bellamy, H.S. *Moons, Myths and Man*, Faber & Faber, London, 1950.

Berlitz, Charles. *The Mystery of Atlantis*, Souvenir Press, London, 1969.

Berlitz, Charles. *Atlantis*, Macmillan, London, 1984.

Braghine, A. *The Shadow of Atlantis*, Aquarian Press, London, 1980.

Budge, E.A. Wallis. *The Gods of the Egyptians*, Dover Publications, New York, 1969.

Cayce, Edgar. *Edgar Cayce on Atlantis*, Warner Books, New York, 1968.

Churchward, James. *The Lost Continent of Mu*, Neville Spearman, London, 1969.

Davies, P. *The Cosmic Blueprint*, Unwin Hyman, London, 1989.

Donnelly, Ignatius. *Atlantis – The Antediluvian World*, Sampson, Low, Marston & Co. Ltd., 1882.

Emery, W.B. *Archaic Egypt*, Penguin Books, London, 1971.

Goodman, Jeffrey. *The Earthquake Generation*, Turnstone Books, London, 1979.

Guirand, Felix (ed.). *Larousse Encyclopedia of Mythology*, Hamlyn, London, 1968.

Hapgood, Charles. *Maps of the Ancient Sea Kings*, Turnstone Books, London, 1979.

Heinberg, Richard. *Memories and Visions of Paradise*, Jeremy Tarcher Inc. Los Angeles, 1989.

Home, Margaret. *The Modern Textbook of Astrology*, Fowler & Co. Ltd., London, 1975.

Hope, Murry. *Practical Egyptian Magic*, Aquarian Press, London, 1984.

Hope, Murry. *Practical Celtic Magic*, Aquarian Press, London, 1987.

Hope, Murry. *The Psychology of Ritual*, Element Books, Shaftesbury, 1988.

Hope, Murry. *The Elements of Greek Tradition*, Element Books, Shaftesbury, 1989.

Hope, Murry. *Ancient Egypt – The Sirius Connection*, Element Books, Shaftesbury, 1990.

Hope, Murry. *Time: The Ultimate Energy*, Element Books, Shaftesbury, 1991.

Hoyle, Fred. *The Intelligent Universe*, Michael Joseph, London, 1983.

Ivimy, John. *The Sphinx and the Megaliths*, Abacus Books, London, 1976.

Michell, John. *The View Over Atlantis*, Abacus Books, London, 1978.

Mooney, Richard. *Colony Earth*, Souvenir Press, London, 1974.

Musaios (Charles A. Musès). *The Lion Path*, Golden Sceptre Publishing, California, 1985.

Muck, Otto. *The Secret of Atlantis*, Collins, London, 1978.

Pisanis, George Ch. (trs. John Alexander). *The Lost Civilization of Atlantis*, Spiritualist Society of Athens, Athens, 1988.

Plato (trs. Desmond Lee). *Timaeus and Critias*, Penguin Books, London, 1977.

Robinson, Lytle. *Edgar Cayce's Story of the Origin and Destiny of Man*, Berkley Books, New York, 1983.

Saurat, Denis. *Atlantis and the Giants*, Faber & Faber, London, 1957.

Scott-Elliott, Col. W. *The Story of Atlantis*, Theosophical Publishing Co., Benares, India, 1896.

Scrutton, Robert. *The Other Atlantis*, Neville Spearman, Jersey, 1977.

Scrutton, Robert. *Secrets of Lost Atland*, Neville Spearman, Jersey, 1977.

Scwhaller de Lubicz, R.A. *Sacred Science*, Inner Traditions International, Rochester, Vermont, 1961.

Sheldrake, Rupert. *A New Science of Life*, Paladin Books, London, 1981.

Spanuth, Jurgen. *Atlantis of the North*, Sidgwick and Jackson, London, 1979.

Spence, Lewis. *The History of Atlantis*, University Books Inc, New York. 1968.

Spence, Lewis. *The Occult Sciences In Atlantis*, Aquarian Press, London, 1968.

Taylor, Stephen & Dee, Nerys. *Atlantis Past and to Come*, Atlanteans Association Ltd, Malvern, 1968.

Tomas, Andrew. *We Are Not The First*, Souvenir Press, London, 1971.

Tomas, Andrew. *Atlantis – From Legend To Discovery*, Robert Hale, London, 1972.

Vigers, Daphne. *Atlantis Rising*, Andrew Dakers, London, 1944.

Warlow, Peter. *The Reversing Earth*, J.M. Dent & Sons, London, 1979.

Wood, David. *Genisis*, Baton Press, Tunbridge Wells, 1985.

INDEX

Ages, Ammonite List of 64-5
air travel 107
Akashic Records 83, 106, 170
Akhantuih 117, 124, 149-51
Alper, Frank 172-3
Americas, the 56
Ammonites 42, 64, 139, 158, 159, 160
animism 122, 134
Antarctica 57
Anthroposophy 170-1
architecture 47-9, 82-3, 101-2
Arien Age 22, 64
asteroids 162
astrology 143-5
Atland 58, 80, 81
Atlantic Ocean 65-8
Atlantis: Myth or Reality 34, 55, 70, 91, 97, 164
Atlantis
  alternative sites of 55-65
  climate of 72-3, 74-5
  description of 44-52, 82-3
  development of (Plato) 47-9
  government of 50, 152
  personal experiences of 173-5
  position of 29-30, 68-71,

73-5
  rising 176-82
  sinking 78, 164-75
  size of 72-3
atomic power 107, 108
axis tilt 12-14, 17, 20, 21, 36, 42, 62, 80, 162, 163
Azores 65, 68, 69, 70

barter system 118-19
bionics 109, 110
black holes 102, 171
blood group, Atlantean 90-4
Braghine, Colonel 76-7, 89, 91, 163
Bull cults 33, 50, 52, 113

calendar, Sothic 144, 158
Cancerian Age, 23, 24, 33, 62, 64, 76
caste system 89
Cayce, Edgar 73-4, 106, 168-9, 177-8
Central America 56-7
channelling 31, 82-3, 165-8, 172
chaos and order 24, 30, 99, 120, 131-2, 140-41, 155, 176, 182
chaos science 19, 31, 76, 163

Churchward, Colonel James 15, 17, 19-20, 24-5, 27-8, 63, 90, 135
civilization, degeneration of 25
climate change 58-61, 81
Codex Cortesianus 18-19
Codex Critias 33, 34-6
Codex Timaeus 33
Codex Troanus 18, 19
colonization
  Atlantean 88, 168
  by Frisians 37-8
  by Mu-ans 24, 27-8
colour, importance of 119, 147, 153, 156
continental drift 12, 14, 59
cosmology 112
Cradock, Phyllis 172
creation myths 86-90
Cro-Magnon man 91, 92
crystals cult 104-7

Dance of the Rising Sun 125, 126-7
Danuih 117, 124, 147-9, 155, 157, 183-6
dates, table of approximate 63-4
Davies, Professor Paul 102, 103, 104
deities 114, 122-5
diet, Atlantean 118

DNA 85
Donnelly, Ignatius 34, 65, 70, 90, 91, 93, 94, 122

Earth, change in orbital position of 79, 80, 82
education 119
Egypt
  history of 32, 38, 40, 41
  old religion of 77, 96, 136-7
  and race 90
  and subtle bodies 138
Emery, Professor 38, 64, 75
energy 104-5, 107, 108-9, 110, 111, 115
epagomenal days 77, 78-80, 144
equidistant cross 15, 136, 137, 147
extraterrestrials 25, 86

Festival of Air 116-17
Festival of Earth 117
Festival of Fire 116
Festival of Water 117
Flood 92, 94, 96, 122, 164
forecasts of Atlantis rising 176-82
  Amerindians 180
  ancient Greek sources 180
  Berbers 180
  Daphne Vigers 178-80
  Edgar Cayce 177-8
  Nostradamus, Mother Shipton, The Fox 181-2
  Tony Neate (Helio Archanophus) 180
Freemasonry 141
Frisians 33, 37, 42, 58, 87, 92

Gaia Hypothesis 21, 163
Geminian Age 22, 62, 64
genes 106
  and Atlantean sinking 165
  Atlantis genetic pool 86
  dilution of divine 53-4
  extraterrestrial 86
  genetic studies 92-3
geological evidence of

Atlantis' position 68-71
geometry, sacred 71, 101
glaciation 58-9, 59-60
Gods of the Four Elements (Table) 136
Gondwanaland 12, 15, 20
government in Atlantis 50, 152
Great Year 21, 22-4

Hapgood, Professor Charles 28, 57, 59, 60, 63, 64, 74, 88, 136, 163
healing 109-10, 121-2, 132, 154-6
height 75, 77
Helio 123, 124
Helio Arcanophus 82, 165-7, 174
Heliona 123, 124, 186
hemisphere, Atlantis' position in 73-5
Hoerbiger, Professor Hans 75-6, 77, 163
Horus, 77, 78, 144
Hoyle, Professor 53, 86
Hymn to the High Sun 125, 128-9

Ice Age 15, 59-60, 62, 88
inhabitants of Atlantis 87, 89
interbreeding 17, 37, 86, 93, 165
Isis 42, 77, 78, 120, 144

Khe-Ta 117, 118, 123, 124, 155, 158
Khiet-Sîn 116, 118, 123-4, 155, 158, 160, 184, 185
Kogi Indians 28-9

land masses, early 12-15
language 91, 97, 145
Lemuria see Mu
Leonine Age 23, 33, 63, 93, 107, 132
Lhasa Record, The 17-18
Libran Age 23, 33, 63, 132
lights, ever burning 110-11
Lovelock, Professor James 21, 163
Lurasia 12, 15

magic
  laws 141-2
  and priesthood 132-3, 141-3
  and science 99, 131-5
Mead, G.R.S. 95-6
metaphysical sources of Atlantean sinking 164
missionaries, Atlantean 89-90
moon
  lunar theories 77, 163-4
  lunar worship 77, 113
  position of 144
  presence of 75-7
  proximity of 75
Mooney, Richard 58-9, 62, 79-80
Mu 12, 15-25, 27-8, 90
  datings for catastrophy of 19-20
Muck, Dr Otto 60, 71, 72, 162-3
Musès, Dr C.A. 143-4
music 125
myth and legend of Atlantean sinking 164

Neate, Tony 31-2, 82-3, 166-7
Nephthys 77, 78, 144
Neters 40, 77, 78, 122, 144, 158
Norse history 38
North Sea 33, 58-63, 81
numbers, importance of 102-3, 135-6

Oera Linda Book 37, 42, 58, 75, 80, 81, 87
order, 132
  see also chaos and order
Order of Passage 120, 155, 156
Osiris 23-4, 42, 77, 78, 140, 144

panspermia theory 53-4, 86
Paradise 94-5
particles 99, 131, 140, 142-3
Penrose, Dr Roger 102, 103
Philaeia 124
Pisanis, George Ch 167-8

Piscean Age 22
Plato 25, 29, 33, 44-54, 72, 163, 164
Pluvial 57, 62, 63, 64
pole shifts 17, 36, 57, 59-60
Poseidon 47, 50, 113, 122
Prayer to the Setting Sun 125, 129-30
Precession of the Equinoxes 21
preselenite age 113, 163
priesthood
  and colour 153
  and healing 121-2, 154-6
  hierarchy 99, 152-3
  and initiation garments 154
  and magic 132-3, 141-3
  and science 98-9
  terrestrial and extraterrestrial duties 157
  training for 99-100, 156-7
see also religion
Primary Four 15

quantum mechanics 100
quasi-crystal 102-4

race 27, 87, 89, 90, 93
  new Atlantean 182-3
religion
  influence in everyday life 117-20
  Mu-an 16
  solar 16, 116-17, 122, 125-30
solar state 113-14
  telluric and cosmic energies in 115-16
see also priesthood
rites

of earth Goddess, Danuih 147-9
for healing and protection of Danuih 183-6
of Judgement 100-1, 125
magical 145-51
of Passage 120
of Protection dedicated to Akhantuih 149-51
of solar religion 125-30
of Union 154

Sacred Four 16, 135, 136, 137, 147
Sahara Desert 57-8, 62
Schwaller de Lubicz, RA 39, 144, 145
science
  in everyday life 101-2
  and magic 99, 131-5
  and priesthood 98-9
Scorpian Age 23-4, 30, 32, 63, 65, 132
sea worship 122
Set 23, 77, 78
Seven Great Commands 16
Shemsu-Hor 38-40, 63, 64
Sirius 32, 54, 102-3, 132, 144, 145, 157-60
solar festivals, four 116-17
solar power 106, 115
solar worship 16, 116-17, 122, 125-30
Solon 34-6, 42, 44
sonics 100, 111, 120
space travel 107, 108
Spence, Lewis 29, 40, 52, 81, 112, 122, 134, 164, 165
spiritual progress 139
spiritual transformations 133

Steiger, Brad 172
Steiner, Rudolf 63, 170-1
stellar influences 20-2
subtle bodies 138-41
sunrise, different 80-2
surgery 109, 111
survivors, Atlantean 31-2
symbology 101, 103, 135-7, 139-40
  Mu-an 15-16

Ta-Khu 116-17, 123, 124
Tartessos 55-6
Taurean Age 22, 52, 64
technology 107-9, 109-10
telepathy 120
Termier, Paul 68
Theosophical Society 169
Thera (Santorini), 55
Theurgy 133-4
Tiahuanaco 57
Time and priesthood 100-1
Timelessness 106, 170, 177
Tomas, Andrew 107, 108-9
transport 121
Tunisia 56

Vedas 88-9
Vigers, Daphne 171
Virgoan Age 23, 63, 82, 114, 132
volcanic deposits 68, 71
Volulpa 81

Warlow, Peter 28, 74, 163
wave 131, 142
Wegener, Dr Alfred 12, 15
West and East Africa 56
winged disk 16, 154
writing, system of 94-7

Yucatan 56-7